D0369919

SHAKESPEARE ALOUD

EDWARD S. BRUBAKER

SHAKESPEARE ALOUD

A Guide to his Verse on Stage

Lancaster, Pennsylvania

Copyright © Edward S. Brubaker 1976
Published by the Author

Manufactured in the United States of America

Fifth Printing 1988

Copies available at $4.25
Order from E. S. Brubaker, 645 North President Avenue
Lancaster, Pennsylvania 17603

ISBN 0-9613496-0-3

822.33
E-1
B886s

ACKNOWLEDGEMENTS

Quotations from Shakespeare's plays are taken from *The Riverside Shakespeare,* 1974, G. Blakemore Evans, textual editor, by permission of Houghton Mifflin Company, publishers.

It is a pleasure to acknowledge the assistance of the staff of the Ashland Public Library, Ashland, Oregon, and the staff of the Fackenthal Library, Franklin & Marshall College, Lancaster, Pennsylvania.

Marian Brubaker and Mary Brubaker gave editorial advice and helped in proofreading. My friends, Hugh Evans, J. William Frey, Ann Hayes, and Gordon Wickstrom, answered questions and provided encouragement.

I owe thanks to my students in Drama 11 who put up with my first fumbling attempts to say something sensible about blank verse, and to the many actors of the Oregon Shakespearean Festival whose work helped so much in making it all sound familiar.

TO MARY

Because – she objects to long hours,
dares to correct my pronunciation,
and can sing the savageness out of a bear.

12-28-90 Emery-Pratt $9.57

PROPERTY OF
METHODIST COLLEGE LIBRARY
FAYETTEVILLE, N. C.

CONTENTS

SHAKESPEARE ALOUD

I

VERSE ON STAGE

> I pray you mar no moe of my verses with reading them ill-favoredly.
>
> – *As You Like It.* 3.2.261-262.

An actor preparing his first Shakespearean role is often troubled by his unfamiliarity with Shakespeare's kind of dialogue. But he soon discovers that the speeches are exciting to study and to rehearse.

Everywhere he sees artifice, the work of an enormously resourceful poet creating and arranging, and yet, the more he studies and works with the dialogue, the less artificial it feels. The human voice colored with human emotion finds its way out of the strange phrases and sentence structures. The play of wit is as natural as it is clever. And when performance time comes around, he discovers that Shakespeare's dialogue supports him at every turn, giving him the stuff he needs to sustain character and action, command attention and interest, and bring an audience to vibrant life.

Actors who have played Shakespeare know that he demands much of them but they know that he was a man of the theatre and placed his art in their service.

His plays should not be thought of as experiments in verse forms, as patterns of imagery, exercises in rhetoric, nor are they studies in themes and theories, nor approaches to existential dilemmas. His plays are scripts for actors. His verse, his rhetoric, his thoughts, his plots, are aids to performance, characterization, motivation, eloquence. However much the professors of criticism, ethics, and current events may find worthy of study in Shakespeare, they cannot claim that Shakespeare wrote for them, mastered his art for them.

The players have long since lost their copyright to Shakespeare's plays and their inheritance has become public property. Now scholars who know little, care less, and think never of the art of acting, write so much about Shakespearean drama from the point of view of their special interests, that all of us forget the theatrical basis of Shakespeare's art.

No wonder actors preparing their first roles in Shakespeare are apprehensive and troubled. In the library and classroom they find an alien, not a familiar figure. a genius so loaded with thought that it doesn't seem possible that he could have had an actor's problems in mind when he wrote. But in the theatre, the actors discover that the genius understood them and set them no impossible tasks. The dialogue, the role, the play, all were made for them.

Certainly this is true when the matter of speaking Shakespeare's verse comes up. An actor with a role written in verse begins with apprehension. He has been told that the basic iambic pentameter line goes like this, da dum da dum da dum da dum da dum. Now if that were even vaguely near the truth, the basic iambic pentameter line is something to fear and avoid. That kind of singsong, humdrum rhythm would certainly rob speech of idiomatic reality and plain sense.

Let us assume the actor is curious and goes to the library. He has to know more. Where do accents fall? Why? What variations are there? What should I be on the look out for? Unfortunately, almost nothing written on the subject bears any relationship to performance.[1]

If an actor consulted a monograph or chapter on the subject of Shakespeare's versification, he might find himself in the middle of a dreary argument as to whether Shakespeare wrote syllabic or accentual verse. That is, whether Shakespeare followed rules which limited the number of syllables to a line or which limited the number of accents to a line. Or whether he wrote both kinds at different times in his career.

Now surely when learned men cannot agree about the general rules which Shakespeare might have followed in writing verse, let alone where the accents fall in a particular line, then an actor cannot learn much to help him in performance by studying their arguments and demonstrations.

Or we might find in the library a discussion of how Shakespeare learned to evade the requirements of regular blank verse and developed a verse form that was almost, but not quite, prose. A verse form so flexible that one cannot tell what it is, but which has subtle modulations of surprising expressiveness. This kind of discussion will interest an actor more, since it depends on aesthetic perceptions. He settles down to read. He may be told that the regular iambic rhythm of the famous line:

x / x / x / x / x / x
To-morrow, and to-morrow, and to-morrow, *Mac.* 5.5.19 [2]

places a heavier stress on the word *and* than would ordinarily be used, slowing the pace of the line and suggesting the weariness Macbeth feels. Or he may be told that the feminine ending, or unaccented final syllable, of the line and in the repeated word, *tomorrow* (x / x), creates a falling, trochaic rhythm which suggests the weariness Macbeth feels. If this subtle inter-play of iambic and trochaic rhythms combine to the same effect, who would care to say what the rhythm of the line is? Or that the terms iambic or trochaic refer to anything very different. The actor is likely to respond, but I know Macbeth is weary, I know it by the situation, the movement of the story, the plain sense of the words. I don't need to analyze the metrics to discover that. It is reassuring that Shakespeare writes so expressively, but I hardly need to scan his lines to know that.

The actor leaves the library feeling that scanning Shakespeare's lines is a subtle, but not a very useful thing to master. He decides to speak the lines according to their sense and let the accents fall where they will. He discovers that the lines work! The rhythms come out. This is because the pattern of accented syllables and the accommodation of the phrasing to the ten syllable line are there to make the sense clear. Shakespeare wrote in verse to support an actor's efforts to be clear and colorful, not to illustrate some theory of prosody or to set up a rhythm in counterpoint to plain sense.

This, it seems to me, is the first thing to know about Shakespeare's verse. And it is a point which is overlooked because we forget what Shakespeare was doing. He was writing scripts for actors. If he was concerned about accents and careful to count syllables, there must have been some valid theatrical reason for it. How does the verse Shakespeare wrote serve the actor? If we keep that question in mind, we may find the reason behind whatever rules he followed and be able to scan his verse with reasonable certainty.

Scanning verse is not a difficult thing to do. It is not the same thing as analyzing poetry. The study of Shakespeare's poetry involves a lot more. In scanning we are simply interested in noticing which syllables in a line of verse are accented and the pattern in which the accents fall.

Doing this generally presents no problem. Anyone who speaks English can scan Shakespeare's verse correctly. This is because a versifier does not write verses which require words to be accented in a way that is different from ordinary speech. He selects words which fit his meter, and if the word doesn't fit, he finds or invents one that does. With few exceptions, saying the word the way we usually do shows us what the verse pattern is.

The few exceptions, and they are very few, arise because Elizabethans sometimes pronounced words differently than we do. For example, we say
/ x /
misconstrued as a three syllable word, putting stress on the first and last syllables. Thus when we scan Shakespeare's line:

x / x / / x / / x /
Alas, thou hast misconstrued every thing. *Caesar.* 5.3.84.

The line does not fit a regular metrical pattern. And when we say it aloud, it
x / x
seems awkwardly phrased. If, however, we say *misconstrued,* putting stress on the second syllable as the Elizabethans did:

x / x / x / x / x /
Alas, thou hast misconstrued every thing.

The line scans in a regular metrical pattern of alternating accented syllables, and we find it much less awkward to say out loud.

But differences in pronunciation of this kind are seldom a problem. The Elizabethans spoke English very much as we do, and only a small number of words in Shakespeare's enormous vocabulary were accented differently than they are in modern English.[3] Generally we can trust our own pronunciation to show us where the accents fall in a line of verse and what its metrical pattern is.

In this case, and in others like it, pronouncing the word the Elizabethan way presents an interesting problem. Although the older pronunciation makes the line less awkward to say, the word *misconstrued* (x / x) is not easily recognizable to modern ears, but *misconstrued* (/ x /) is recognizable. Should we use the older pronunciation and have the advantage of a flowing line of verse, or the modern pronunciation and have a recognizable word? I think the answer in most cases, is to opt for the recognizable, modern pronunciation.

The problem occurs because the two advantages of verse are in conflict. Verse permits a line to be said rapidly without confusion and makes words clearly recognizable to the ear. We can't have both if the accentuation of a word has changed since Shakespeare used it in a line of verse.

Putting dialogue in regular verse serves two practical purposes in the theatre. It provides the actor with dialogue which is easy to speak rapidly and clearly. And it provides the audience with certainty about what they are hearing. That double function of verse in the theatre is the important principle which underlies Shakespeare's versification. This essay explores his verse from that point of view.

There are possibly some other practical advantages in verse dialogue. Verse is probably easier to memorize than prose. But learning lines is not nearly so difficult a task as the theatrically naive suppose, so that the trouble of putting dialogue in verse seems hardly worth the little advantage it would give the memory. Other possible advantages in verse dialogue are that it is more vigorous and sounds more exciting, and that it casts an aura of ritual solemnity about the proceedings on stage. If these seem to be plausible statements, we should consider as well, that some very exciting dialogue exists in prose, and that prose is the language of the most solemn rituals.

But if the practical advantage of verse in the theatre is that it makes dialogue easier to speak and easier to hear, that is no trivial consideration, particularly in a theatre like Shakespeare's where dialogue has an importance over spectacle that it seldom claims or needs in the modern theatre.

Placing value on such basic matters as hearing and speaking, is not to say that Shakespeare's verse, in some mysterious way, is not also the foundation of complicated poetic achievements. It is simply to begin at the pedestrian roots.

To do this we must use our ears, rather than our eyes. So much modern verse is written for reading rather than for recitation that we are accustomed to staring at a printed page until we get a poem. This habit has led us to forget that good verses to Shakespeare were verses which could be heard and said, verses that suited the voice and ears, that could be caught in the mind as they flew by. Shakespeare's verse repays the closest study with the eye, but it was written for the ear.

Modern literature reaches us almost exclusively through the printed page and we find it odd that in an age before printing, when literature was made for public recitation, verse was the medium of nearly all imaginative writing. Our fictions are addressed to readers alone and silent in chairs. Writers no longer have a need for verse, and readers seldom notice whether they are reading prose or verse. If we remember that Shakespeare's audience was literate, but accustomed to conducting their affairs by listening and speaking rather than by reading and writing, we may see more accurately why verse was so commonly used. And understand, too, how the Elizabethan audience managed to attend and enjoy plays which are so difficult to read.

And now the reader must be warned on two points. First, the discussion of accent which makes up the second chapter in this book is rather dry, but it is fundamental and cannot be avoided, although everyone may not need to read it. It would have been clearer and more exactly written if the technical language and symbols used in linguistic study had been employed. But these are not generally known and I am not as familiar with them as I should be. Despite these shortcomings, the discussion of accent is basic because it seeks to make clear that accent in verse is not different from accent in ordinary speech and that accent is of great importance in conveying meaning. If these points are already understood and granted, the reader has permission to skip to the third chapter.

The reader must be warned, secondly, that the discussion of verse presented here is no magic key for the correct speaking of verse. The discussion points out in innumerable ways that verse is based on the way our language is ordinarily spoken. And the surest way to speak it well is to know all we can about our language. This takes listening as much as reading. Just as we learn to act by observing people, so we learn to speak by listening to them. Training will sharpen our powers of observation, make us more conscious of what we see and hear, and of what we ourselves are doing, but it will not give us a magic key to sudden understanding.

Training helps us to acquire knowledge and technique. To possess them we need practice. And that means for one thing that all the examples cited here must be read out loud. They must be heard, not skimmed with the eye.

Reading this book will, I think, clear the air. There are so many vague fears associated with the matter of speaking verse. They amount to superstitions. The strange belief that only the elite know how to handle the matter correctly has got to be undermined. The bullying and cowardice that has developed around the idea of a standard, correct speech in our culture is enough to make the angels weep. Shakespeare's use of language is a source of such enormous pleasure, it seems worthwhile to open the matter of his verse to fresh thinking based on observation.

If there is a traditional lore about the way verse must be handled in the theatre, I must confess that I have not been able to find it or meet anyone who knew it. The art of speaking verse well is not hidden. It can be mastered by anyone who listens, thinks, and practices.

II

THE USE OF ACCENT

> That any accent breaking from thy tongue
> Should scape the true acquaintance of mine ear.
> – *King John.* 5.6.14-15.

Since the writing system used for English does not mark accented syllables, we are inclined to think of accent as an incidental element to the sound of words. And we overlook the effect accent has on our ability to recognize words by ear.

In reading, of course, the eye doesn't need accent marks to recognize words. Once in a long while, however, the deficiency of our way of writing shows up. A word in print puzzles us because we cannot tell where the accent falls. The sentence, *We refuse no refuse,* for example, would not be puzzling if the accented syllables in *refuse* were marked, *We refúse no réfuse.* But examples of this kind are hard to find. Our writing system works very well without accent marks because the eye has plenty of other clues to help it recognize words.

In listening, however, when the ear alone must do the work, accent is relied on heavily. Since Shakespeare's theatre verse was written for the ear and not for the eye, it may be helpful to listen more closely to the effect of accent on words. Once that is clearly in mind, the place of accent in verse may be more precisely understood.

One way to notice the effect of accent is to take an ordinary word and compare the changes in its sound when accent is arbitrarily shifted from one syllable to another. Take, for example, the word, *tomatoes.* If we place an accent on the
/ x /
first and last syllable, the word becomes very strange to the ear, *tom-a-toes.* When the accent is on the middle syllable, we immediately recognize the word. It doesn't matter too much if the vowels and consonants are a bit different. One
x / x x / x x / x x /
can say, *ta-mayt-as, ta-maht-as, ter-mayt-ies,* or even, *ta-mayts,* as long as the accent falls on the second syllable, the word is recognizable although it may be noticeably different from the way we usually say it or are accustomed to hearing it.

The point is that the placement of accent has a great effect on the way a word sounds, and as far as the ear is concerned, the arrangement of accented and unaccented syllables is a prominent and distinctive feature of a word. Accent is not something that floats about looking for a syllable to land on according to the speaker's whim. It is fixed by usage as stubbornly as any element of language.

As a part of human culture, language is subject to change and variation. At any one time there are a few polysyllabic words undergoing change in accentuation. Until the new pronunciation establishes itself, those words will be accented in two ways and be recognizable in both pronunciations. In modern
/ x x /
American speech, *banal* is accented, *ban-al* by some speakers and, *ba-nal* by others. In such cases listeners recognize the word said either way. They may have a prejudice against the pronunciation they do not use themselves, but they recognize the word they feel is mispronounced. But once a particular accentuation is used by a large majority of cultivated speakers, the other accentuation disappears and the ear loses its flexibility of response. Then only the accepted pronunciation makes the word easily recognizable.

Shakespeare's contemporaries would apparently recognize the word, *revenue* whether accented on the first or second syllable. In the same play, *Richard II,* the verse at one time requires the word to be accented in the modern way, with accent on the first and last syllable:

> x / x / x / x / x /
> The revenue whereof shall furnish us *R II.* 1.4.46.

And at another time, the accent falls on the second syllable, requiring a pronunciation probably equally recognizable to his audience, although it strikes us as strange:

x / x / x / x / x /
My manors, rents, revenues I forgo; *R II.* 4.1.212.

Shakespeare himself probably felt that was a better pronunciation, for he placed *revenue* in verse so that it required that accentuation more often than the accentuation that has prevailed in modern English. He used the word, in the singular and plural form, in 17 lines of verse; 11 times the accent falls on the second syllable, 6 times on the first.

Nowadays the accent has been fixed on the first syllable of *revenue,* and it is often pronounced as a two syllable word; our ears don't catch the word when the second syllable is accented. [4]

In the theatre, by the way, audiences will tolerate an occasional strangeness of pronunciation. They enjoy a few things being odd in a play. They don't expect every word to be pronounced their way, nor even to get every word. And since Shakespeare's verse very rarely requires a different accentuation than the one we would ordinarily use, an actor will not try the patience of a modern audience if he occasionally uses a pronunciation which is strange to them.

To return to the effect of accent on the ability to recognize words by ear, let us look more closely at what happens when the accent moves from one syllable to another. Take the words we have been discussing, *refuse, tomatoes, banal,* and *revenue.* Here they are, spelled and hyphenated in a way which may help to visualize the change in syllables, depending on whether they are accented or not:

x /	x / x	/ x	/ x /
re-fuse	ta-mayt-as	bane-al	rev-e-nue
/ x	/ x /	x /	x / x
ref-use	tom-a-toes	ba-nahl	re-ven-ue

Presenting the words in this form may exaggerate what happens, but it shows two things that should be kept in mind. First, it shows that the distinctive features of a syllable change noticeably when the accent falls on it or is removed. The syllables when accented have distinctive vowels and tend to include more consonant sounds. By contrast, when unaccented, syllables have an indefinite vowel, or schwa, and fewer consonant sounds. A change in accent placement changes the color and shape of the syllables and is bound to make a word difficult to recognize by ear.

Second, the list of words illustrates our tendency to pronounce words by alternating accented and unaccented syllables. If the word begins with an accented syllable, the second syllable is unaccented, the third accented, and so on. If the first is unaccented, the second will be accented, the third unaccented, and so on. In most dictionaries a distinction is made between syllables which have a primary and those which have a secondary accent. For purposes of scanning verse, however, this distinction is not needed. It must be understood, of course, that all accented syllables are not said with equal energy, and they are marked accented only in relationship to the syllables that surround them. Similarly, unaccented syllables in verse are not all equally weak.

Before passing from this consideration of accent in words to a discussion of accent in larger sound structures, such as phrases, clauses, and sentences, one more observation should be made about the influence of accent on the sound of words. The point is this: A clear differentiation between accented and unaccented syllables gives a word its distinctive sound.

Consider a case of someone saying a word like *independent* indistinctly. He
/ / / /
is asked to repeat it. So he very carefully says, *inn-dee-pend-dent,* putting equal stress on all the syllables. This may help his listener to visualize syllables, but it doesn't come close to showing what the word sounds like in ordinary speech. The speaker over-compensates. Where at first he said the syllables with so little energy that the accented ones did not stand apart from the others, the second time he gave the unaccented syllables equal strength. In both instances the sound and feel of the word was distorted. To the ear a clear differentiation between
/ x / x
accented and unaccented syllables, *ind-e-pend-ent,* gives the word its characteristic and recognizable sound.

This suggests that something important, as far as hearing is concerned, happens when words are placed in regular verse. The metrical pattern reenforces the distinction between accented and unaccented syllables. The words are therefore easier to recognize since their characteristic sound becomes more evident. More so than in prose. In the context of regular verse, the listener, or I should say, his ear anticipates the order of the accents, and the speaking voice, falling into the rhythm, gives the accented syllables that extra energy which sets them apart. The ear catches the words without confusion.

Just as accent differentiates syllables in words, so it helps to differentiate words in phrases, clauses, and sentences. Here accent helps the ear to identify the function and grammatical relationship of words, the key to the meaning of a sentence. Accent only helps in this important process, and because it does not play the crucial role that word order does, we do not often notice the role of accent in the process.

In most cases the grammatical relationship of words in an English sentence is indicated by word order. The major elements of sentences – subjects, predicates, objects, modifiers – can be expressed by single words or by complicated constructions, but in an English sentence the arrangement of those major elements is a standardized arrangement conforming to a small number of sentence patterns. In reading English we rely heavily on those standard sentence patterns to guide us to the structure and meaning of the sentence.

In listening to English, the structure of the sentence is also signalled by intonation patterns, or sentence tunes, which underscore the patterns. Thus beside the accented or emphasized words, the ear notices both the word order and the accompanying intonation. Accent, then, is only part of the complicated signals by which the ear gets hold of the meaning of a statement. Although accent, or emphasis as it is commonly called in a sentence, only reenforces our perception of the relationship of words, occasionally accent plays a crucial role in helping us catch the meaning of a sentence. [5]

As far as speaking verse is concerned, the accentuation of words in phrases, clauses, and sentences is, therefore, every bit as important as the accentuation of syllables in words. Perhaps it is more important. A variation in the way syllables are accented may make it hard to recognize a word, but a variation in the relative emphasis given to different words in a sentence will change the meaning of the sentence.

Everyone is familiar with this fact, but it would be helpful to get it more clearly in mind. The most important element in a sentence is the predicate, and it always gets a stronger emphasis than any other element. Or to put the matter another way, accent shows us where the predicate is.

In the simplest English construction of noun and verb, as in the sentence,
x /
John ran, the accent falls on the predicate, not on the subject. The difference in relative stress is slight, but if the accent were reversed so the sentence sounded
/ x
like this, *John ran,* the construction no longer tells what John did, but which boy ran. Its predication has changed. That kind of idea would be more clearly

expressed in writing by using a construction which places the predicate in the latter part of the sentence, *The runner was John.*

The predicate is often expressed by words other than verbs. Thus in a sentence like this, *He made pies,* the object of the verb carries the principle idea and gets a relatively stronger accent. In this sentence, *He ate lunch,* the accent on the verb makes it the predicate. In both cases, a change of accent would change the meaning of the sentences, and the function of the words.

Similarly, adverbs may sometimes be the most important part of the predicate and get a stronger accent. A sentence like, *He ran fast,* has a different meaning when accented this way, *He ran fast.* And nouns and adjectives placed in the predicate by a linking verb function as predicates, *He is king,* and *He is old.*

Aside from indicating which part of the predicate is significant, accent differentiates adjectives from the nouns they modify. Word order which places the adjective first, usually makes this clear, but a slight difference in accent reenforces the distinction. In phrases like, *green house* and, *dark room,* the distinction is noticed when the accent is reversed. *Greenhouse* and *darkroom* are heard as compound words, not as phrases made up of an adjective and noun.

It will occur to some, who have not consciously listened to the way of accents in spoken English, that emphasis in such phrases can be placed on the adjectives. If I say, *The dark room was empty,* darkness is emphasized and, unless I am talking about photography, the context will keep the phrase from being misunderstood as a compound word. But the thing to notice is this. If darkness is the more important idea, the sentence would be phrased like this, *The room was dark and empty.* This places the adjective *dark* in the predicate and in an emphatic position. The general rule holds, adjectives are less important than the words they modify. They are emphasized by tedious actors who want others to be more impressed by what they say than they are themselves.

One final example of how accent reenforces our perception of the function of words in a sentence should be mentioned. Words like *in, by, on, up,* and so forth, when used as prepositions are given less stress than the words they join to the sentence: *in time, by force, on top, up hill.* But those same words function as parts of a verb in many phrases, and then they are more strongly accented than the verb: *come in, drop by, go on, drink up.* In these cases, word order makes these relationships clear – the accented word follows the less important one – but accent underscores the relationship and function. When used as genuine prepositions, they claim no accent; when used as part of the verb, they are accented.

There is no point in enumerating more of the ways accent is used to bring important elements of a sentence into prominence and to keep less important ones in the background. Enough has been said to indicate how accent aids the ear in recognizing words, their function in language structures, and thus in catching the meaning of sentences.

How all this applies to verse in the theatre needs further discussion. The distinction between accented and unaccented syllables is often very slight. Unless we give it conscious attention, we often have trouble deciding which one of two syllables or two words is more strongly stressed. Indeed one of the principle difficulties in scanning verse arises because we are not accustomed to noticing those slight distinctions which are made and heard unconsciously in speech. And one advantage of scanning verse is that the poet teaches us about those distinctions.

Moreover, when sentences are in verse the speaking voice tends to make those slight distinctions more clearly. For example, take the sentence, *I am so sad.* It is probable, because of word order and sense, we would place major emphasis on *sad.* It is clearly the predicate. But what is the relative emphasis of the other syllables? If the words are placed in verse, as in this line:

x / x / x / x / x /
In sooth, I know not why I am so sad; *Merchant.* 1.1.1.

we get a more definite idea of the relative stress given to each word. The distinctions between accented and unaccented syllables are clearer. The distinctions are slight, but enough to give the words a precise relationship and meaning. Both actor and audience are assured of a precise meaning.

Prose can offer no such assurance. Relying entirely upon word order and the sense implied by it, the actor speaking prose can feel as confident that his accents fall at significant places, but since his voice is not supported by a regular rhythm, the audience cannot anticipate the fall of accents and cannot be as certain of what they hear.

These notes on accent suggest that placing accented and unaccented syllables in some regular verse pattern enhances an audience's ability to hear, and, as a corollary to that, supports an actor's efforts to be clear and to project a precise meaning.

In passing we have also noticed that there is a general tendency for English words to be pronounced by alternating accented and unaccented syllables. This is a matter of some importance to versification which will be discussed in the next chapter.

One further point should be noticed. In the various constructions just discussed, the accent nearly always comes in the latter part. Because English word order nearly always determines that important words are placed in the latter part of a construction. This is particularly noticeable when phrases of two one-syllable words are listened to. Consider these examples:

x /
Verb and adverb – run fast

x /
Subject and verb – John ran

x /
Verb and adjective – is dark

x /
Adjective and noun – green house

x /
Preposition and noun – in time

There are constructions where the latter position is not the more important one, but by and large, the word order of English phrases and sentences places the important element last. Accent reenforces that. Another way of expressing this point is to say that English phrasing is generally climactic, the emphasis falls in the latter part of the construction. This correctly suggests that the iambic measure, one in which an unaccented syllable is followed by an accented one, is the easiest metrical pattern to use in English verse.

In these notes I have tried to show how verse makes speech more distinct than it ordinarily is by magnifying, or rather, megaphoning the difference between accented and unaccented syllables, and between the more important words and the subordinate and auxiliary ones.

If verse so enhances speech, it may well be asked why any theatre dialogue is written in prose. The answer is that men don't talk in verse in ordinary life, and if the scene is given over to something like a realistic imitation of life, prose is the language that gives that effect. There are values, however, in artifice, theatricality, distinction, which are sometimes more important. And when such values preside over the scene, verse is the most effective medium of expression. And though good verse is built and patterned on the language men use, it necessarily dresses that language in artfulness and style.

Shakespeare and the theatre he worked in seem to have found no conflict in the development of prose and verse scenes in the same play. A performance of his plays, responsive to their wide range of effect from the height of style to the plain idiom of common life, requires the mastery of both forms of dialogue.

As far as accent is concerned, the principles which determine accent in verse are no different from the principles which operate in prose dialogue. And in fact, one of the advantages of scanning Shakespeare's verse is that it makes us more conscious of the role of accent in daily speech, something we do not notice in routine reading and writing. In scanning we also come to realize that Shakespeare, however poor he may have been as a speller according to modern standards, had a very good ear. He knew how men spoke.

In the description of blank verse which follows, a verse form that is particularly suited to the English language will be discussed. It has already been suggested that a regular alternation of accented and unaccented syllables and a general iambic movement would provide a verse that would go trippingly on the English tongue. But there is more to it than that.

III

VERSE FOR ENGLISH

And gave the tongue a helpful ornament,
– *I Henry IV.* 3.1.123.

Shakespeare's lines are most commonly written in iambic pentameter. The English for that is blank verse. As technical descriptions these terms are helpful, but we must understand that they describe his verse only in the most general way.

More of his lines scan as iambic pentameters than as anything else, and most of them are unrhymed or blank verses. But Shakespeare hardly writes a scene in verse without rhyming some of his lines. And his lines are not always in five measures or pentameters, nor are his measures always iambic, a two syllable measure with an accent on the second syllable.

Perhaps we should be wary of terms adapted from classical prosody like iambic pentameter, for English is not Latin or Greek. And just as the terms of Latin grammar get in the way of understanding English grammar, so the terms of classical prosody may cloud our understanding of verse written by a master of

English. If we begin with the assumption that Shakespeare tried to write iambic pentameters, we may get an impression that he failed, or gave it up as a bad job. It might be better to begin with the assumption that what he did was exactly what he wanted to do.

Shakespeare wanted to write verse of practical use to actors on stage, not a verse that imitated a particular pattern. If we remember that, we may be able to describe and understand the principles of his verse accurately.

Now English is a language that fits most easily into a verse pattern very like iambic pentameter. And it is probable that if Shakespeare had never heard of iambic pentameter he would have written verse closer to that than to anything else simply because he wrote English. In this chapter I want to show why I think that is so. In the following section, the peculiarities of the verse Shakespeare wrote will be described in greater detail.

The opening line of *The Merchant of Venice* is unusually regular, perhaps because it is made of monosyllables and contains one complete statement. Here it is, marked and divided into the five iambic feet:

x / x / x / x / x /
In sooth, / I know / not why / I am / so sad;

The division into measures or feet, corresponds almost exactly to the phrasing of the sentence. In other words, a pause could be taken at the end of each foot. Further, each foot can be described as iambic, that is a two syllable measure with an accent on the second syllable. The end of the line completes a statement, or unit of thought, and could be marked with a period. [6]

Few lines hit the ear so clearly as regular blank verse. Saying it rapidly without thinking what it means could easily produce the deadly sound of da dum da dum da dum da dum da dum. The next line in the same speech sounds quite different and has a very different rhythm, although it conforms technically to the verse pattern and can be scanned in the same way:

x / x / x / x / x /
It wear/ies me,/ you say / it wear/ies you;

The line includes two parallel and contrasting statements which set up a rhythm that gives a feeling of two, rather than of one line:

It wearies me,
You say it wearies you;

But however different in feeling from the first line, it scans as a regular blank verse. The five measures are iambic and a major unit of thought is completed at the end of the line.

If every line exactly fitted the description of having ten syllables with alternating accents, blank verse would remain a remarkably varied verse form. Consider the following examples and how different they are in sound, tempo, texture, and intonation:

> A horse, a horse! my kingdom for a horse! *R III.* 5.4.7.
> She lov'd me for the dangers I had pass'd, *Othello.* 1.3.167.
> Methought I heard a voice cry, "Sleep no more! *Mac.* 2.2.32.
> The barge she sat in, like a burnish'd throne, *Antony.* 2.2.191.

Those lines all scan as regular blank verse, but the varied length of words, and the pauses between them come at such different places that the rhythm is never steady as a drum beat, and the pulse of the beat is never of the same intensity.

Even the most regular line, whether punctuated or not, has a variety of pauses in it. English simply cannot be spoken straight on for ten syllables. And the pauses themselves are of various lengths. If we use a slash for a slight pause, a double slash for a longer one, and a triple slash for a full stop, the two lines from *The Merchant of Venice* could be marked like this:

> In sooth / I know / not why / / I am / so sad / / /
> It wearies me / / / you say / it wearies you / / /

Considering the variety of pauses, the movement of these lines is not alike.

Another source of variety, perhaps evident enough not to need mentioning, is that the accented syllables are not given equal stress, nor are the unaccented ones equally light. If we mark the relative intensity of stress in the accented syllables by using numbers from 1 to 5, the lines might be marked like this:

```
  2       3         4 1       5
In sooth, I know not why I am so sad;
   4        1      2       3     5
It wearies me, you say it wearies you;
```

Here again, a close look reveals that the lines are not alike. Except for one similarity which may seem coincidental, but is not. The final words in each line receive the heaviest stress. We'll come back to that.

But even the weighing of relative stress in the accented syllables does not show the variety of accent in a line. The unaccented syllables are sometimes given more stress than words which are accented. Take the first line:

> x / x / x / x / x /
> In sooth, I know not why I am so sad;

In the third measure *not* is unaccented in comparison to *why,* but *not* is probably given more stress than *sooth,* the accented syllable in the first measure, and more stress than *am,* the accented syllable in the fourth measure. In the second line:

> x / x / x / x / x /
> It wearies me, you say it wearies you;

The first *it* probably is stressed more heavily than *say,* the accented word in the third measure. On the other hand, *it* in the fourth measure is so lightly said that if it were not for the unmarked but necessary pause after *say,* the vowel would elide in speech, combining the words so they would sound like *say't.*

In short, for purposes of scansion, accent is a relative, not an absolute matter. We don't mark a syllable accented if it comes up to a certain level of intensity; we mark it accented if it is simply stronger than the other syllable in its measure.

Because of the variety of stress given the syllables and the variety in length and placement of pauses, depending on the words and their phrasing, blank verse can be said to be a verse form that allows considerable variety in rhythm, pacing, and sound. There is nothing necessarily monotonous about it. A poor writer may write dull blank verses, but the rules of the form should not be blamed for that. Perhaps a longer passage in regular blank verse may help to make the point. Here is the dying speech of Warwick from *The Third Part of Henry the Sixth:*

> The wrinkles in my brows, now fill'd with blood,
> Were lik'ned oft to kingly sepulchres;
> For who liv'd king, but I could dig his grave?
> And who durst smile when Warwick bent his brow?
> Lo, now my glory smear'd in dust and blood!
> My parks, my walks, my manors that I had,
> Even now forsake me; and of all my lands
> Is nothing left me but my body's length.
> Why, what is pomp, rule, reign, but earth and dust?
> And live we how we can, yet die we must. *III H VI.* 5.2.19-28.

The speech composed of Anglo-Saxon monosyllables is rather vigorous and emphatic. The voice predictably marches right up to the tenth syllable of each line, lands on it heavily, pauses, then marches through the next line. This gives the speech a stiff formality which suits the character, the situation, and the sentiments expressed. The stiffness can give way to a more colloquial sound if the actor varies the length of the pauses and the intensity of the accents within the line. But even without that kind of study, the speech can be effective theatre. The thoughts, however, are rather commonplace and repetitive, and that, quite aside from the regularity of the lines, makes the speech less interesting than what we expect from Shakespeare.

Here is a speech by the dying Hotspur in *The First Part of Henry the Fourth.* The lines are similarly regular, as far as verse form is concerned, but the speech has a colloquial and immediate intensity:

O Harry, thou hast robb'd me of my youth!
I better brook the loss of brittle life
Than those proud titles thou hast won of me.
They wound my thoughts worse than thy sword my flesh.
But thoughts, the slaves of life, and life, time's fool,
And time, that takes survey of all the world,
Must have a stop. O, I could prophesy,
But that the earthy and cold hand of death
Lies on my tongue. No, Percy, thou art dust,
And food for – *I H IV.* 5.4.77-86.

Aside from the interesting break in the flow of the last line, marking the moment when Hotspur dies, the verse is as regular as in the speech of Warwick. If it is more interesting, it is because the ideas are less conventional, not because the regularity of the verse has been altered.

So far we have discussed blank verse within the limits of a simplified working description. A line of ten syllables, divided into five measures in which an unaccented syllable is followed by an accented one. The lines of Warwick and Hotspur fit that description exactly. But blank verse is not so simple. The first and last measures of the line were regularly treated by Shakespeare and other Elizabethan playwrights in a different way. We need to examine that and other matters before our description of blank verse can be adequate.

In the meantime we can examine some of the ways in which blank verse suits the English language, within the terms of our simplified description.

First, it can be pointed out that English is a strongly accented language. The difference between an accented and an unaccented syllable is a more noticeable difference than in some other languages, French, for example. A verse form which regularly alternates accented syllables suits such a language. This is because accented syllables cannot be said one after another without a pause between them, or without the relaxation of tension which an unaccented syllable allows. A sentence like *The black board broke* is difficult to say because the three final one syllable words are all nearly equally stressed. On the other hand, a sentence like this, *The blacker board is broken* can be said much more easily and swiftly because a lighter syllable comes between accented ones. The voice cannot keep hitting accented syllables without relaxing or taking a pause. Accenting a syllable with the voice is like hitting a piano key with a finger, you can't strike again until you relax. The alternate accented and unaccented syllables allow rapid and flowing speech.

All of Warwick's lines, for example, move easily except the line:

Why, what is pomp, rule, reign, but earth and dust?

The trouble with the line is that three words, *pomp, rule, reign,* have the same grammatical function and claim a correspondingly equal stress. But the line can be said without awkwardness if *rule* is more lightly stressed:

x / x / x / x / x /
Why, what is pomp, rule, reign, but earth and dust?

When it comes to unaccented syllables placed side by side, the situation is somewhat different. Consider the varied measures in these lines:

x / x x / x x / x x /
Why, all his behaviors did make their retire

x x / x x / / x / x x /
To the court of his eye, peeping thorough desire: *Love's.* 2.1.234-235.

The words move very rapidly and compel the speaker into a tripping and artificial rhythm. But notice how the pause after *eye* is forced on the speaker by the accent in *peeping* placed right next to *eye.* Two unaccented syllables placed side by side, speed up speech; two accents side by side, force the speaker to stop.

x x /
Notice too, that the two unaccented syllables in the phrase, *of his eye,* will combine, unless the speaker is very careful, and will sound like, *of's eye.* This tendency of English speakers to combine two unaccented syllables when they occur side by side is checked by a variety of things, which will be discussed in the sections on elision in the next chapter, but, just as we find two accented syllables

difficult to say side by side without taking a pause between them, so we find it difficult to sound two unaccented syllables without combining or slurring them.

One more note. Three accented syllables and three unaccented syllables cannot be said. English speakers are so accustomed to an alternation of accented and unaccented syllables that they simply cannot say three equally stressed syllables in a row. A phrase like *pomp, rule, reign* will be said, *pomp, rule, reign* or *pomp, rule, reign.* The distinction will be slight, but it will be there. Similarly we cannot say *council of the king.* The phrase will come out *council of the king.* We automatically speak by alternating accented and unaccented syllables whenever we can.

In sum, the alternation of accented syllables is a characteristic of blank verse which suits our strongly accented language.

Another characteristic of blank verse which suits our language is the iambic measure. As has already been pointed out in the last chapter, the phrasing of English generally requires important words to be placed in the latter part of a phrase, clause, or sentence. Thus the ordinary movement of a grammatical unit is from less important elements to the ones needing emphasis. The final word is often an emphatic one. The voice gathers power as it moves to the close of a phrase or the period of a sentence. Considering this, and the advantage to English speakers of an alternation of accented and unaccented syllables, then the measure most suited to English speech would be iambic, where the accent falls on the second of two syllables.

But a rigorously regular use of iambic pentameter lines creates a problem which should be noticed. The speech of Warwick quoted above illustrates the problem. There nearly every line is a sentence, or an important clause, so the pause at the end of the line is strongly marked, coming at the end of a unit of thought. This places a strong emphasis on the final word of each line. And, indeed it would be difficult to avoid that kind of emphatic end to the line as long as each line is a unit of thought and the final syllable is accented. Now, while this kind of end to the line is probably an advantage in the dialogue of a boisterous play like *Henry the Sixth,* in other plays the persistent heavy fall on every tenth syllable can be a problem.

Shakespeare and his fellow playwrights of the Elizabethan age had an alternate way of treating the closing measure of a line of verse which alleviated the problem. Instead of stopping every line with an accented syllable, they sometimes used an extra unaccented syllable in the final measure, giving the line eleven rather than ten syllables. The third line of *The Merchant of Venice* illustrates the practice. The extra syllable is marked by parenthesis:

> x / x / x / x / x /(x)
> But how I caught it, found it, or came by it,

The line is comparatively less forceful at the end. The technical term *feminine ending* for the unaccented final syllable may be appropriate, but the addition of the extra syllable does not necessarily create a retiring or relaxed feeling. These lines I think remain vigorous, although they have a feminine ending:

> x / x / x / x / x / (x)
> Believe me, no. I thank my fortune for it,
>
> x / x / x / x / x / (x)
> My ventures are not in one bottom trusted, *Merchant.* 1.1.41-42.

Certainly the jolting effect of stopping every line on an accented syllable is softened by this variation. Elizabethan playwrights used the eleven syllable line so often that it might make more sense to describe blank verse as a ten or eleven syllable line, beginning with an unaccented syllable, and with an accent on every other syllable. But this description doesn't quite do.

The writers of blank verse had yet another variation, and it too had the effect of lightening the heavy emphasis on the end of the line. This time they changed the opening measure. They began with an accented syllable, reversing its position with the unaccented syllable in the first measure. The opening line of *Richard the Third* illustrates the practice:

> / x x / x / x / x /
> Now is the winter of our discontent

A reversal of the accented syllable in the first measure appears so often in blank verse passages that it should not be regarded as a momentary departure from the regular pattern for the sake of variety, but rather as characteristic of blank verse. Here are some further examples:

> / x x / x / x / x /
> Glory grows guilty of detested crimes, *Love's.* 4.1.31.
>
> / x x / x / x / x /
> Plucking the grass to know where sits the wind, *Merchant.* 1.1.18.
>
> / x x / x / x / x /
> Doom'd for a certain term to walk the night, *Ham.* 1.5.10.

These reversals of accent in the first measure often give a striking and energetic opening to the line. Beginning the line strongly runs counter to the general tendency of English phrasing to begin quietly and to rise in energy as it moves to the close. Instead of every line beginning that way, when a reversal is used, some of them spring from the starting position, relax, and then gather energy again.

The sound and feel and movement of lines depends, of course, on more complex matters than the placement of accented syllables. Reversing the accent in the first measure, or adding an extra unaccented syllable in the final measure, while tending to make the end of the line less emphatic and heavy footed, does not invariably produce that effect. The reversal of accent does not always draw attention to the first measure. And the feminine ending does not always soften the final measure.

Besides, it is not accurate to speak of these variations from the strict iambic pattern as occuring only at the beginning and end of lines. They are likely to occur at any noticeable pause in the flow of speech, whether within the line or at the end, and whether the pause is a grammatical one or one introduced by an interruption. Significant pauses occur most frequently at the end of a line, where a unit of thought is completed, thus the extra unaccented syllable is most often introduced there. And the reversal of accent often comes in the first measure because it follows the pause at the end of the previous line. But the point is that whenever the flow of speech is interrupted, a corresponding interruption in the regular alternation of accented and unaccented syllables could be introduced.

Thus an extra unaccented syllable occurs within a line as well as at the end:

x / x / x / (x) x / x / (x)
So let it be with Caesar. The noble Brutus *Caesar.* 3.2.77.

x / x / x / (x) x / x /
And by opposing, end them. To die, to sleep – *Ham.* 3.1.59.

And the reversal of accent can come at the beginning of a sentence, or after a break or interruption of a sentence within a line:

x / x / x / / x x /
The greatest is behind. Thanks for your pains. *Mac.* 1.3.117.

x / x / x / / x x /
My Lady Grey his wife, Clarence, 'tis she *R III.* 1.1.64.

And finally, both variations from the iambic pattern can occur in the same line:

/ x x / x / x / x / (x)
Something is rotten in the state of Denmark. *Ham.* 1.4.90.

x / x / x / / x x / (x)
To be, or not to be, that is the question: *Ham.* 3.1.55.

/ x x / x / / x x /(x)
What shall Cordelia speak? Love, and be silent. *Lear.* 1.1.62.

Now these lines are not strictly iambic pentameters. However, although they are exceptional and unusual, they represent standard practice in blank verse writing. The measures which are not strictly iambic occur at particular places according to rule. The measures that begin with an accented syllable [/ x] occur after a pause, that is, at the beginning of a new line, clause, or sentence. The measures that have an extra unaccented syllable [x / (x)] occur before a pause, that is, at the end of a line, clause, or sentence. In short, a break in the regular iambic measures and, what amounts to the same thing, a break in the regular alternation of accented syllables, occurs only at a pause in speech. Not always, of course, but not otherwise.

The value of this to an actor is not hard to understand. If the speech flows with a regular sequence of accented and unaccented syllables, he knows he will be able to speak rapidly and clearly, assured that a break in rhythm will not occur when sense requires continuity.

A break in the flow of alternating accented syllables can help to mark the phrasing of a sentence, particularly in keeping parallel phrases and clauses, or items in a series, separate from each other:

/ x x / x / x / x /
Sweet are the uses of adversity,

/ x x / / xx / x /
Which like the toad, ugly and venomous,

x / x / x / x / x /
Wears yet a precious jewel in his head;

x / x / x / x / x /
And this our life, exempt from public haunt,

x / x / / x x / x /
Finds tongues in trees, books in the running brooks,

/ x x / x / x / x /
Sermons in stones, and good in every thing. *As You.* 2.1.12-17.

/ x x /
Then shall our names,

x / x / x / x / x /
Familiar in his mouth as household words,

/ x x / / x x / x /
Harry the King, Bedford and Exeter,

/ x x / x / x / x / (x)
Warwick and Talbot, Salisbury and Gloucester,

/ x x / x / / x x / (x)
Be in their flowing cups freshly rememb'red. *H V.* 4.3.51-55.

Despite the irregularity of these lines, the number of measures is consistently held to five, and the departures from the iambic pattern come only in the measures before and after pauses. Notice too that the five measure line consistently contains a grammatical unit. The pause at the end of the line is caused by the fact that a unit of thought has been completed.

Using the line as the unit of thought is an important feature of any system of versification. The lines may be of varied lengths in different verse forms, but the phrasing must be adjusted to a set number of measures for the artifice of verse to be noticed. Thought may overflow from one line into the next, and some sentences may reach a period within a line, but even when that happens, some sort of pause occasioned by the end of a phrase will be reached at the end of the line.

In the case of blank verse, the number of measures in a line is five. Five measures seems to be the easiest number for the English language to be adjusted to. Using six measures as the unit of thought tempts a writer to pad his statements, and using four measures cramps his statements into epigrams. The five measure line suits the speaking voice as well. It may be too long for a musical phrase, but for dialogue it is most convenient. Four measure lines, while suitable for songs, are difficult to speak with any sense of flow.

Now it should be noticed that the feeling that we are listening to blank verse comes largely from the line being treated as the unit of thought. The pauses that come from the structure of the sentence, the natural pauses we take as a phrase, clause, or the sentence itself is completed at the end of the line, give the clearest impression of measured speech. The way to make verse evident to the ear is to pause at the end of the line. The accentuation pattern is not so important in this regard.

Sometimes, of course, the units of thought spill from one line into the next, and the sense of where the line ends will be difficult to hear. In such cases, the verse form tends to be concealed and much less evident than in speeches where each line has a noticeable pause at the end. Consider these lines, and how seldom a major pause comes at the end of the line:

Our revels now are ended. These our actors
(As I foretold you) were all spirits, and
Are melted into air, into thin air,
And like the baseless fabric of this vision,
The cloud-capp'd tow'rs, the gorgeous palaces,
The solemn temples, the great globe itself,
Yea, all which it inherit, shall dissolve,
And like this insubstantial pageant faded
Leave not a rack behind. We are such stuff
As dreams are made on; and our little life
Is rounded with a sleep. *Tempest.* 4.1.148-158.

The periods all come in the middle of the line, and although there are natural pauses to be taken at the end of every line, the sense overflows the line, rather than being noticeably contained within it. It is unmistakable and glorious poetry, but if the verse form is to be evident, the actor has to exaggerate the pause separating line from line. [7]

There is no rule to guide an actor in deciding how evident to make the verse form in speaking lines. That is, deciding how consistently he takes a pause at the end of the line or how noticeably he makes that pause. Some of Shakespeare's verse is quite formal, artificial and theatrical. It is hardly possible to speak such verse without making the lines stand apart as units of thought. And some of his verse is realistic, idiomatic, and informal. The lines follow the uneven and unpredictable flow of thought, rather than the formal rhetorical organization of an oration. In such cases, the units of thought spill into the next line, or stop short of the full line, and the pauses within the line are sometimes more important than those at the end. Obviously it is a matter of taste and tact, not of right and wrong to decide whether a formal or realistic manner of speech is to be used. The rules and ways of accentuation can help the actor very little in making such decisions. The voice naturally follows the accent pattern in blank verse to the pause, what we do then is another matter.

Finally, it should be pointed out that the difference between English prose and blank verse is not a striking difference. The major features of blank verse, its five measure line and its general iambic movement, allowing a regular alternation of accented with unaccented syllables, make it a verse form easily adaptable to our language. And prose writing, especially when used for public speeches, comes very close to being blank verse. Lincoln's Gettysburg Address, for example, if lined according to its phrasing, would look like this:

> Fourscore and seven years ago
> our fathers brought forth upon this continent
> a new nation, conceived in liberty,
> and dedicated to the proposition
> that all men are created equal.
> Now we are engaged in a great civil war,
> testing whether that nation, or any nation,
> so conceived and so dedicated,
> can long endure.

Enough of the Address has been quoted to make the point. The average number of syllables in the first 8 lines, is 10. And the iambic movement is predominant in every line. There is a fairly regular alternation of accented and unaccented syllables. A practiced versifier would have little difficulty in turning that speech into blank verse.

By way of summary, we can describe blank verse as follows: The line consists of five measures. The measures are iambic, except that sometimes the measures that begin a line, sentence, clause, or phrase, start with an accented syllable, and sometimes the final measure of a line, phrase, clause, or sentence, has an extra unaccented final syllable.

Almost invariably, and with reliable consistency, Shakespearean verse conforms to this description. Very often in scanning we will find a line that appears not to fit this description, but if we remember that Shakespeare wrote for the speaking voice and was aware of the contractions which mark our speech, we will find that a seeming irregular line is regular when spoken. The next chapter goes into the matter of contractions in ordinary speech and in Shakespearean verse.

IV

THE SHAKESPEAREAN LINE

You find not the apostraphas, and so
miss the accent.

– *Love's Labor's Lost.* 4.2.119-120.

Those who have followed the discussion so far and those who have skipped to this page, would both probably be willing to read a summary and restatement before going further into the thicket of special problems connected with scanning Shakespeare's verse.

The argument has been that a pattern of accented syllables makes dialogue easier to hear and to speak. The verse of Shakespeare, therefore, has a practical value in the theatre.

If the actor wants to communicate, the verse pattern is there to help him. This is fundamental. Shakespeare's verse is not more or less beautiful than his prose. But it is better for the ear. It can be said rapidly without confusion and it can be heard with greater certainty. When an actor works with the accentual pattern his audience recognizes words and their function in a sentence easily;

they relax with the assurance they know what is going on. When he works against the accentual pattern (which, by the way, should be hard to do), a jumble of unrecognizable and unrelated syllables will puzzle the audience; they gradually give up trying to figure out what the noise means. In a theatre so dependent on the spoken word as Shakespeare's, that means disaster.

As a corollary to this, it must be recognized that the accentual pattern in verse dialogue is not an arbitrary thing that must be decided about according to vague aesthetic, esoteric, or arbitrary principles. The plain, literal, common way of saying words and phrasing sentences is the surest guide to a correct observance of accent in verse. Accent derives from the relative stress given to syllables in words and the relative emphasis given to words in sentences. It is not something made up and added on, like frosting on a cake, it is inherent in the way we speak.

Accent is so intimately involved in the way words convey meaning that a careful consideration of what a line means will be as accurate a guide to where the accents fall as scanning lines according to a theory of what the metrical pattern should be. But the reverse is also true, scanning lines can help us to see what the possibilities of meaning are.

This is not to make any large claim for the value of knowing how to scan Shakespeare's verse. It is no magic key to unlock secret meanings, much less a ticket to success on the stage. Scanning lines is somewhat like analyzing their grammar – useful on rare occasions. But just as one does not need to know about grammar to speak grammatically, so one does not need to know about scanning verse to observe the accentual pattern in speaking verse. One does it naturally, that is by force of habit developed when we first learn to speak and sustained by daily practice. Knowing how to scan does not change our habits, it simply makes us more aware of what they are.

But it can be claimed that scanning Shakespearean verse is interesting, and if it has little practical value, it is rewarding to get a closer look at part of what lies in back of his extraordinary and arresting command of our language.

Shakespeare's blank verse can be described as follows. The line has five measures which are usually iambic [x /]:

x / x / x / x / x /
Uneasy lies the head that wears a crown. *II H IV.* 3.1.31.

x /x / x / x/ x /
The quality of mercy is not strain'd, *Merchant.* 4.1.184.

Sometimes the measure that begins a line, sentence, clause, or phrase, starts with an accented syllable [/ x] :

/ x x / x / x / x /
Striving to better, oft we mar what's well. *Lear.* 1.4.346.

/ x x / / x x / x /
Words without thoughts never to heaven go. *Ham.* 3.3.98.

Sometimes the measure that ends a line, sentence, clause, or phrase, has an extra unaccented syllable [x / (x)], and a line containing such measures could have as many as 11 or 12 syllables, rather than the usual 10:

x / x / x / x / x / (x)
I come to bury Caesar, not to praise him. *Caesar.* 3.2.74.

x / x / (x) x / x / x / (x)
My father's brother, but no more like my father *Ham.* 1.2.152.

The same line may include both variations from the standard iambic measure:

/ x x / x / x / x /(x)
Free from the bondage you are in, Messala; *Caesar.* 5.5.54.

/ x x / (x) / x x / x / (x)
Let me not think on't! Frailty, thy name is woman! *Ham.* 1.2.146.

This description of Shakespeare's blank verse applies to the verse he wrote for ordinary dialogue. It excludes such special forms as the rhyming dialogue of his early comedies, and the speech of fairies and witches and others who do not talk as ordinary people do. After allowance is made for these exceptions, it will be found that Shakespeare's blank verse is written according to principles followed with some strictness. The basic line of five iambic measures prevails, and the two variations of the iambic measure are introduced according to principle, not according to whim.

The fundamental principle is to accommodate sentence structures to the limited syllables of the line, completing units of thought at the end of the line and introducing new units at the beginning. Some units, of course, end and others begin within the line, but the stop and start of the line is also the stop and start of a grammatical phrase, or, to describe the same thing in different terms, the stop and start of a unit of thought. Running through the units of thought is a regular alternation of accented and unaccented syllables. When the flow of a phrase comes to a pause, or is interrupted, the regular alternation of accents may also be interrupted. Thus the regular pattern of accents can be said to tie the words of a phrase together, like a slur in music, and a break in the pattern of alternating accented syllables, can be regarded as part of its grammatical pointing or punctuation. Departure from the iambic measure is not made for the sake of variety, but to help reveal the structure of the sentences.

There are lines which do not scan according to the patterns shown above, nor according to the principles which have just been described. But before we look at them, the largest problem connected with scanning must be examined, the problem of contractions. Until we train our ears to notice them, many of Shakespeare's lines which scan regularly will not appear to do so.

Contractions

Contractions occur in ordinary speech more frequently than we may be aware of. We do not notice them for a number of reasons. For one thing our spelling conventions require that words usually be spelled out in full, even those that are pronounced in a shortened form most of the time. For example, the word *interest* is nearly always said as a two syllable word, "int'rest", but almost invariably spelled as a three syllable one. Thus in reading and writing we see words in their fullest form and are not likely to notice the shortened form they take in the context of speech.

And because teachers of formal writing mark contractions as colloquial in red ink, most of us have acquired a prejudice against colloquialisms in speech, although that is precisely where they belong. We superstitiously believe that they are not quite proper and that using them betrays an uneducated or slovenly person. Nearly everyone, for example, pronounces the name *Margaret* as a two syllable word, "Marg'ret", but many will insist that the only correct form is, "Mar-gar-et". The assumption that only the most stilted and careful pronunciation is correct is a false one that has to be put aside when we scan Shakespeare's verse. This may not be very easy to do because the same teachers who have taught us to write and pronounce in a formal manner have also taught us that Shakespeare is a great and classic author. It becomes difficult to believe that great and classic authors are not also formal writers whose works demand formal speech.

This belief is aggravated by a peculiar fact of theatre history. It used to be that Shakespearean actors were trained or apprenticed in a system of elocution which was extremely formal. Words were carefully, lovingly, and fully treated. Enough of that tradition lingers to lead many to suppose that Shakespearean verse requires a special and different manner of pronunciation, something more solemn and ponderous than we would hear about us in everyday life.

We need to remember that dialogue for the theatre derives vitality and authenticity from speech, not from writing. Shakespeare had a fine ear for the way men speak. He lived in an age when school marms and masters scolded their pupils about Latin pronunciation and when English, as the living language, was wisely allowed to take care of itself. Shakespeare modeled his verse on what he heard, not on what he had been told was correct.

In scanning his verse we need to forget the prejudices and assumptions we have about what should be there and look for what is there. In the matter of colloquial contractions we will discover that we speak much the same language. Although contractions are very seldom indicated by spelling or by apostrophes in a Shakespearean text, they are taken into account. Here are some examples:

"int'rest" for *interest*

x / x / x / x / x /
He hath more worthy interest to the state *I H IV.* 3.2.98.

"Marg'ret" for *Margaret*

x / x / x / x / x /
O Margaret, Margaret, now thy heavy curse *R III.* 3.4.92.

"degen'rate" for *degenerate*

x / x / x / x / x /
His noble kinsman – most degenerate king! *R II.* 2.1.262.

"virt'ous" for *virtuous* and "rev'rend" for *reverend*

x / x / x / x / x / (x)
She is a virtuous and a reverend lady, *Errors.* 5.1.134.

"be'ng" for *being*

x / x / x / x / x /
An honest tale speeds best being plainly told. *R III.* 4.4.358.

"partic'lar" for *particular*

x / x / x / x / x /
That I should love a bright particular star *All's Well.* 1.1.86.

It might be considered, for the moment, that some of these contractions are allowable by poetic license, granted to a versifier, but unlikely to occur in ordinary speech. It can be shown, however, that the contractions are almost unavoidable when those lines of verse are spoken. A glance at the list of examples reveals that the conditions in which contractions occur can be described by a specific rule: *A word contracts when it is placed in a phrase so that two relatively unaccented syllables occur side by side. When this happens, the vowel of the weaker of the two unaccented syllables is cut out, or elided, which shortens the word.*

Further explanation may clarify this rule and show why it works. Take the word *degenerate* which appears in its shortened form in the third example listed above. It is a four syllable word ordinarily, that is, when it is considered all by itself, or listed in a dictionary, or placed in an emphatic position. For example in this line, used as a predicate adjective, it has importance and would be pronounced as four syllables:

x / x / x / x / x /
To show how much thou art degenerate. *I H IV.* 3.2.128.

When placed in the phrase, *degenerate king,* however, the ordinary accentuation of the word makes the phrase awkward to say because it brings two accented syllables side by side, *degenerate king.* When this is said out loud, with energy to reach an audience, the speaker will find that he has to take a pause between those accents, like this, *degenerate – king.* This is awkward, unless you want to make *king* sound heavily ironic, but even then the pause suggests that the speaker can't think of what he wants to say.

If we try to get around the awkwardness by not accenting the word *king,* the phrase would sound like this, *degenerate king,* and the relationship of the two words would be muddled. *King* being a substantive modified by *degenerate,* it should receive the strongest emphasis in the phrase. And if the last part of the phrase is not accented, we get the impression that the speaker has lost interest in what he has to say.

When we keep in mind the importance of the word *king* to the meaning of the phrase, we find ourselves saying *degen'rate king* automatically. For if we try accenting the phrase this way, *degenerate king,* we would have to take a pause between the two unaccented syllables, *er - rate,* which gives the word a labored and ponderous pronunciation. However, in saying the word right on without a pause, we find the two unaccented syllables reduced to one and we have said willy-nilly:

x / x / x / x / x /
His noble kinsman – most degen'rate king!

Or, to describe more precisely what has happened, the vowel of the weaker syllable is dropped out, or elided, and the word is thereby shortened.

We are so accustomed by our language to a regular alternation of accented and unaccented syllables that we avoid phrasing which places two accented or two unaccented syllables side by side. When this is unavoidable, we tend to shorten or contract a word so that regular alternation can prevail.

All this is done by force of habit, automatically and unconsciously. It is only when words are quite unfamiliar to us that we have any difficulty in adjusting our accentuation and pronunciation of them to the phrasing in which they occur. For example, we find it disconcerting to discover that the family name of the hero in *Titus Andronicus* has four syllables in one context:

x / x / x / x / x /
Andronicus, would thou were shipp'd to hell, *Titus.* 1.1.206.

and three syllables a few lines later in the same scene:

/ x x / x / x / x /
Titus Andronicus, for thy favors done *Titus.* 1.1.234.

This does not show that Shakespeare couldn't or wouldn't make up his mind about the pronunciation of his hero's name. It shows that he remembered that the number of syllables in a word is variable depending on the context in speech. If *Andronicus* were a familiar name to us, we would have heard those two pronunciations somewhere before we came across the word in verse. We would not, for instance, take exception to a versifier treating a name like *Roosevelt* as a two
/ x
syllable word, *Roos'velt,* in one context and as a three syllable word in
/ x /
another, *Roosevelt.*

We habitually contract polysyllablic words in a pinch, dropping out a weak syllable if that will make the phrase go trippingly on the tongue. In Shakespeare's text as in most writing, the words that would be contracted in speech are seldom marked by an altered spelling, nor is an apostrophe used to indicate the elided vowel. Marks of contraction are unnecessary. Any native speaker would adjust his pronunciation without having to be signalled to do it. And consider as well that the necessary adjustment is all the more likely to be made when a verse pattern reenforces our inclination to speak with a regular alternation of accented and unaccented syllables. It is when we look at the lines instead of saying them out loud, that the contractions seem devised for the sake of the verse rather than consistent with the way English is ordinarily spoken.

Elision between Words

Although we think of words as separate groups of sounds, in speech their separation is not always perceptible. A phrase like, *the United States,* nearly always sounds like, "thu-nite-ed-states." We hear four syllables rather than the five that are there when the words are considered separately. The contraction occurs because the same conditions which cause elision within words operate between words. Two unaccented syllables come side by side, *the united,* and when spoken the weaker vowel drops out, so the phrase becomes, *th' United States.* We are all familiar with similar elisions in phrases like *he's, I can't go, you'll see,* because they are among the few contractions which are allowed to be used in formal writing.

In verse elisions of this kind are more likely to be marked by an apostrophe than they are in prose. Here are some examples:

> Sh' adulterates hourly with thine uncle John, *John.* 3.1.56.
>
> And whipt th' offending Adam out of him, *H V.* 1.1.29.
>
> Th' unkindest beast more kinder than mankind. *Timon.* 4.1.36.
>
> As flies to wanton boys are we to th' gods, *Lear.* 4.1.36.
>
> O, swear not by the moon, th' inconstant moon, *Romeo.* 2.2.109.

In many cases, however, elisions are not marked in Shakespeare's text. He probably never bothered to mark them in the first place, assuming correctly that elision would occur automatically once the actor had memorized the lines. Scanning reveals how aware Shakespeare was of elision in our speech. In the following examples, the syllables that are likely to combine are underlined with a tie bar and the elided vowel is left unmarked:

> Stir up the Athenian youth to merriments, *Dream.* 1.1.12.
>
> To enforce these rights so forcibly withheld. *John.* 1.1.18.
>
> I had rather be a dog, and bay the moon, *Caesar.* 4.3.27.
>
> He brings great news. The raven himself is hoarse *Mac.* 1.5.38.
>
> To crown my thoughts with acts, be it thought and done: *Mac.* 4.1.149.
>
> Showing we would not spare heaven as we love it, *Measure.* 2.3.33.
>
> I tax not you, you elements, with unkindness; *Lear.* 3.2.16.
>
> Against the irregular and wild Glendower, *I H IV.* 1.1.40.

Some of those lines may seem awkwardly phrased when first read, but if spoken rapidly, the underlined syllables will be found to combine by elision of the weaker of the two vowels. And the lines will have gained speed and energy.

Many who write about Shakespeare's blank verse assume that irregular lines introduce a departure from the expected pattern which makes for pleasing variety. Those who make this assumption would argue that the last example quoted above should be scanned this way:

x / xx / x / x / x / (x)
Against the irregular and wild Glendower,

Scanned this way the irregularity of the line reenforces the idea of Glendower's ungovernable wildness. But I think that is too nice a point. The force and speed of the line is reenforced by elision, and that is what an actor would prize. When conditions are right, elisions occur naturally in speech unless an actor makes a conscious effort to avoid them. Departure from an expected pattern does introduce pleasing variety in lyric poems, but stage dialogue becomes tedious when phrases are interrupted by a break in the pattern of alternating accents.

The conditions under which elision occurs need to be more fully considered. Elisions which combine two words do not always occur when two unaccented syllables are placed side by side in a line of verse. In cases where the meaning requires a pause between words, or the speaker simply takes a pause, the interruption in the flow of speech will prevent the pair of unaccented syllables from being combined.

Consider this line:

/ x x / x / x / x /
Smooth runs the water where the brook is deep, *II H VI.* 3.1.53.

A pause would be taken after *runs* because of the inverted word order. The subject *water* follows the verb *runs* instead of taking its usual position before the verb. A departure from normal word order also introduces a pause in this line after the word *costly:*

/ x x / x / x / x /
Costly thy habit as thy purse can buy, *Ham.* 1.3.70.

In addition to pauses caused by the phrasing, others are required by certain consonants. Their sounds are usually represented in English writing by the letters, t, d, b, p, g, and k. These stop consonants are sounded by blocking the breath for an instant with the tongue, lips, or glottis, and this process introduces a stop or pause in the flow of sound. In this line, for example, the sound of *t* in *what* is made by a stop with the tongue which prevents the pair of unaccented syllables from combining:

/ x x / x / x / x /
See what a rent the envious Casca made; *Caesar.* 3.2.175.

And in this line the sound of *d* in *and,* a stop also made with the tongue, prevents elision:

/ x x / x / x / x /
Time and the hour runs through the roughest day. *Mac.* 1.3.147.

Aside from the pauses required by phrasing or by the pronunciation of stop consonants, an actor may take a slight pause to prevent elision although the circumstances for elision are all present. For example, in these lines the pairs of unaccented syllables would combine if the lines are spoken rapidly, but the actor, of course, can avoid elision if he wants to stick to the ten syllable line:

/ x / x / x / x /
Life is as tedious as a twice-told tale *John.* 3.4.108.

/ x / x / x / x /
Time shall unfold what plighted cunning hides, *Lear.* 1.1.280.

/ x /x / x / x /
For the apparel oft proclaims the man, *Ham.* 1.3.72.

We assume these lines were meant to have ten syllables and the possibility that a vowel might be elided was overlooked. Suppose for a moment that an actor were to ask Will Shakespeare, "Shall it be, 'For th' apparel oft proclaims the man,' or 'For the apparel'?" He would probably answer, "Why 'tis all one. Either way the words are understandable and easily said." Besides, the regular alternation of accented syllables is preserved in one reading and the norm of the ten syllable line is preserved in the other.

Although the rules which govern Shakespeare's versification are necessarily stated in rigid form, rigidity in practice cannot be expected. The actor needs to contribute the voice. Scanning will show him how a line might be said, but it would not invariably decide the matter for him.

And there are many times when scanning itself is ambiguous. Here is a line which could be scanned in several ways, all of which obey the rules:

Canst thou not minister to a mind diseas'd, *Mac.* 5.3.40.

The eleven syllables can be reduced to ten by eliding so that *to a* becomes *t'a,* or by contracting *minister* to *min'ster.* Then, the first and second words could be

/ x x /
accented, *Canst thou,* or *Canst thou,* which gives four different ways the line might be said, and each one would obey the rules. Among these possibilities an educated guess would be:

> / x x / x / x / x /
> Canst thou not minister to a mind diseas'd,

But the best educated guess does not settle the matter. The situation developed in performance determines the reading that is finally used. A satisfactory scansion for one production, even for one performance, may be unsatisfactory for another. Some lines, like the crimes of Macbeth, must be acted ere they may be scann'd.

Contraction of Final Syllables

The subject of contractions and elisions cannot be concluded without noticing that some contractions which are almost invariably used in modern English, were sometimes not used by Shakespeare. The word *diseased,* for example, is nearly always spelled *diseas'd* in the folio text, but in one instance it is spelled and meant to be pronounced as a three syllable word:

> x / x /x / x / x /
> Diseased nature oftentimes breaks forth *I H IV.* 3.1.26.

A full pronunciation of the final *-ed* syllable was not done much more often in Shakespeare's speech than in ours, but since it was done at times when we don't expect it, we have to be on the look out for it. Here are some other examples:

> x / x / x / x / x /
> And death's pale flag is not advanced there. *Romeo.* 5.3.96.
>
> x / x / x / x / x /
> Albeit unused to the melting mood, *Othello.* 5.2.349.
>
> x / x / x / x / x /
> I bear a charmed life, which must not yield *Mac.* 5.8.12.
>
> x / x / x / x / x /(x)
> To gild refined gold, to paint the lily, *John.* 4.2.11.
>
> x / x / x / x / x /
> To be so baited, scorn'd, and stormed at. *R III.* 1.3.108.

Notice in the last example that an apostrophe marks the elision in *scorn'd* and that the final syllable is spelled out in the words where it is to be pronounced. In the folio text and in some modern editions, elisions of the final *-ed* syllable are marked by an apostrophe, and if the syllable is to be pronounced it is spelled out. In other modern editions an accent mark is placed over an *-ed* syllable that should be pronounced. But in many editions scanning the verse is the only way of telling whether the vowel is to be elided or not.

In most cases a line will be noticeably less awkward to say if the final *-ed* is sounded when the verse pattern requires it. But there are other oddities of Shakespearean accentuation which would seem awkward and affected if introduced on the modern stage. It is curious to discover, for example, that the repeated words *ambitious* and *honorable* in Mark Antony's funeral oration scan as four syllable words:

> x /x / x / x /x/
> But Brutus says he was ambitious,
>
> x /x /x /x /x /
> And Brutus is an honorable man. *Caesar.* 3.2.86-87.

But those pronunciations would not be acceptable on the modern stage. Antony's ironic repetition of those words would seem heavy handed rather than cunning and subtle. On the other hand it is probably helpful to know that *interred,* in the same oration, can be said as three syllables:

> x / x / x / x / x /
> The good is oft interred with their bones; *Caesar.* 3.2.76.

Here the full pronunciation is not too strange and the line flows more easily.

Another oddity of Shakespearean pronunciation is the occasional full pronunciation of the final *-ion* syllable, as in these lines:

> / x x / x /x /x/
> Seeking the bubble reputation *As You.* 2.7.152.
>
> x / x / x /x /x/
> Such tricks hath strong imagination, *Dream.* 5.1.18.
>
> x / x / x /x / x/
> The brightest heaven of invention! *H V.Pro.* 2.

Notice in these examples that the *-ion* syllable comes at the end of the line, so that if the modern pronunciation were used, the line would have nine syllables rather than ten, but the line would not be awkward to speak because its pattern of alternating accents would not be disturbed. More frequently than otherwise the modern contraction of the final *-ion* syllable is required in Shakespeare's verse:

> x /x /x / x /x /
> Suspicion always haunts the guilty mind; *III H VI.* 5.6.11.
>
> x / x /x /x /x /(x)
> And thus the native hue of resolution *Ham.* 3.1.83.
>
> x / x /x /x /x /
> By bare imagination of a feast? *R II.* 1.3.297.

Elision of the V Sound

While it is a general rule that modern English uses more contracted forms than Elizabethan English, there are some contractions used then which are no longer common. Of these a group occurs so frequently that any one interested in scanning Shakespeare's verse should be aware of it. When the letter *v* is found in a medial position, the sound was often dropped to contract the word. Some common words that meet this condition are *even, ever, never, over, evil, devil, seven, eleven,* and *heaven.* In modern English we know the contractions *e'en, e'er, ne'er,* and *o'er,* but they are part of poetic diction, the treasury of words used to write doggerel verse, not part of our speech. When Hamlet says,

> Horatio, thou art e'en as just a man
> As e'er my conversation cop'd withal. *Ham.* 3.2.54-55.

The contractions *e'en* and *e'er* seem to us affected and formal, not relaxed and familiar. Dropping the medial *v* is simply not done in modern English.

But it was done in Elizabethan times and very often such two syllable words as *even, devil, evil, seven, eleven,* and *heaven* are treated as one syllable words and meant to be so pronounced in the verse of Shakespeare. The words are sometimes puzzling to scan because the elision of *v* is often not marked by an apostrophe, as the following examples will show:

x / x / x / x / x /
Cut off even in the blossoms of my sin, *Ham.* 1.5.76.

/ x x / (x)
Not in the legions

x / x / x / x / x /
Of horrid hell can come a devil more damn'd

x / x / x /
In evils to top Macbeth. *Mac.* 4.3.55-57.

x / x / x / x / x /
From Athens is her house remote seven leagues; *Dream.* 1.1.159.

x / x / x / x / x /
Upon the platform 'twixt aleven and twelf *Ham.* 1.2.251.

x / x / x / x / x /
Nor heaven nor earth have been at peace to-night. *Caesar.* 2.2.1.

Modern audiences may not have trouble recognizing *e'en* for *even, de'il* for *devil,* or *se'en* for *seven,* but they probably would have trouble with *e'il* for *evil, ele'en* for *eleven,* and *hea'en* for *heaven.* Using the modern pronunciation, although it makes the verse irregular, is probably wise. Here again, scanning according to rules can guide the actor, but it should not always decide the matter for him. The purpose of the verse pattern is to make speech clear, if it doesn't do that it should be abandoned.

Anomalies

In scanning Shakespeare's verse we will find some lines which depart from the rules of blank verse. Some are Alexandrines, that is, they have six, rather than five measures:

x / x / x / x / x / x /
To look upon my sometimes royal master's face. *R II.* 5.5.75.

/ x x / x / x / x / x /
Supposition all our lives shall be stuck full of eyes, *I H IV.* 5.2.8.

x / x / x / x / x / x /
I pray thee stay with us, go not to Wittenberg. *Ham.* 1.2.119.

Some have four rather than five measures:

x / x / x / x /
Earth gapes, hell burns, fiends roar, saints pray, *R III.* 4.4.75.

x / x / / x x /
Must give us pause; there's the respect *Ham.* 3.1.67.

/ x x / x / x /
'Gainst my captivity. Hail, brave friend! *Mac.* 1.2.5.

Others have trochaic [/ x] instead of iambic [x /] measures:

/ x / x / x / x / x
Then the whining schoolboy, with his satchel *As You.* 2.7.145.

/ x / x / x / x / x
Ay, or drinking, fencing, swearing, quarrelling, *Ham.* 2.1.25.

/ x / x / x / x / x
Towards their project. Then I beat my tabor, *Tempest.* 4.1.175.

These iambic six and four measure lines, and the trochaic five measure lines are very rare in verse dialogue. Shakespeare almost invariably sticks to the rules.

Some of his lines, however, are irregular and present puzzles to scanners. Sometimes he asks for an elision which seems to violate the rules. Would not the following lines be less awkward if the underlined elisions marked by apostrophes were not observed?

/ x x / (x) x / x / /
Madness in great ones must not unwatch'd go. *Ham.* 3.1.188.

/ x / x / x / x /
Th' expedition of my violent love *Mac.* 2.3.110.

The elisions must have been intended because someone put the apostrophes there. But why? These puzzles are listed because it is important to realize that not all of Shakespeare's lines will scan as regular blank verses, however those rules might be defined. For the most part, however, puzzles in scanning are not created by anomalous or irregular lines. Sometimes we are uncertain of what we hear. And scanning is also a matter of analysis as well as of hearing. The mind and the ear do not always agree. Puzzles that arise from this disagreement can often be explained by dividing lines into measures.

Analysis by Measures

Scanning verse is not entirely a matter for the ears to decide. The mind does the analysis. Sometimes the mind and ear will seem to be at odds. Here is a famous line which the ear tells us should be scanned like this:

```
 /      x  x    /  x       / (x)   x   /       / (x)
Life's but a walking shadow, a poor player,      Mac. 5.5.24.
```

That gives a good picture of what we hear. But the line is much more regular than that. Divide it into measures, and we get this scansion:

```
 /      x     x   /       x      /      x    /    x      / (x)
Life's but / a walk / -ing shad / -ow, a / poor player,
   1            2          3           4          5
```

The ear rejects this because *poor* is so much stronger than *a* in the phrase, *a poor player.* It seems absurd to mark *poor* as unaccented. But the point is that *a* is in the fourth measure, and *poor* is in the fifth. *Poor* is stronger than *a* but they are not in the same measure and are not to be weighed against each other.

This line seems almost impossible to scan in a way that is satisfactory to the ear:

```
  /     x  x   / x   x  /  / x      /
Made to run even upon even ground,      John. 2.1.576.
```

But divided into measures its regularity will be plain:

```
  /    x     x   /     x   /     x   /     x    /
Made to / run ev / -en up / -on ev / -en ground,
   1          2        3        4        5
```

The word *upon* is said and heard as *upon* (marked x / above the word), but since its first syllable is in the third measure and its last syllable in the fourth measure, it is scanned in a way that seems to contradict its pronunciation. Scanning, unfortunately, does not always show the pronunciation of a word, it shows the relative strength of two syllables in the measures in which they occur.

One more seemingly irregular line:

/ x x /(x) x / / x /
Finish, good lady, the bright day is done, *Antony.* 5.2.193.

Now look at it in measured form:

/ x x / x / x / x /
Finish / good lad / -y, the / bright day / is done,
1 2 3 4 5

Bright is said with much more emphasis than *the* but the words are in different measures. The ear may not hear it that way, but the forward, driving movement of the iambic measure is preserved.

This example could be measured and scanned in two ways. As four measures, the scansion looks like this:

x / x /(x) x / x /
The fault, / dear Brutus, / is not / in our stars, *Caesar.* 1.2.140.
1 2 3 4

And as five regular measures:

x / x / x / x / x /
The fault, / dear Brut / -us, is / not in / our stars,
1 2 3 4 5

Which more accurately reflects the versification depends on the relative strength of *in* in the fourth measure.

All this may make scansion seem contrary to common sense. But the point that it might be useful to remember is that the regularity of Shakespeare's verse, demonstrated by analysis, and suggested by the ease with which the lines can be said, doesn't always sound like regularity to the ear.

V

THE RATTLING TONGUE

What pace is this that thy tongue keeps?
– *Much Ado About Nothing.* 3.4.93.

An important assumption on which this study is based is open to question and it might be worth the time to examine it more closely. The assumption is that Shakespeare's verse is regular, that it conforms to the rules of blank verse with remarkable consistency. This assumption may lead us to discover that his verse is more regular than it really is. There is no way of getting around that kind of circularity in argument. We find what we look for. If we believe that regularity in verse is useful in the theatre, we may have a more sophisticated reason for assuming that Shakespeare wrote regular verse than is usually offered, but the assumption still leads us and determines what we shall find. But let us follow for a moment where the argument leads. What is the relationship of verse dialogue to other conventions of the theatre? Consider first the effect that verse dialogue has on a production.

Perhaps Shakespeare had the effect of blank verse in mind when, in the final scene of *A Midsummer Night's Dream,* he has Duke Theseus draw a contrast between a nervous speaker who forgets his practiced accents and a pompous orator who uses

> the rattling tongue
> Of saucy and audacious eloquence. *Dream.* 5.1.102-103.

These words are not flattering but they describe, I think, the general effect of regular and flowing blank verse. It is exciting. Very often it is slick, glittering, and full of itself, but never bumbling, cramping, or tedious. In other words it is artificial and theatrical to the last syllable. The theatrical conventions blank verse was designed to exploit must have been rather different from the realistic conventions of the modern theatre.

Modern scholarship has done much to reconstruct the conditions under which Shakespeare worked and the theatre in which his plays were first produced.[8] The general features of their production system can be summarized like this. There were no long periods of rehearsal, which would make complicated business and stage movements difficult to achieve. Stage directors in the modern sense were unknown. Scenery, that localized the setting or contributed a supporting visual or spacial design, was not used. The language of the plays was complex, metaphorical, richly suggestive, and artificial. Much depended on the actor as a speaker. The audience had to listen in a way they do not have to listen in the modern theatre. They went "to hear a play" rather than to see it.

One curious detail which scholarly research has found difficult to explain, is that productions in the Elizabethan theatre lasted about two hours. In the modern theatre this is nearly impossible without extensive cutting. Shakespeare's shorter plays, *The Comedy of Errors, Macbeth,* and *The Tempest* have about 2,000 lines, but the average is very close to 3,000 lines. This suggests that Elizabethan actors spoke at a clip of 1,500 lines an hour. Modern actors can manage about a 1,000 lines an hour, which seems quite brisk to us.[9] What would happen if we took our pace up another notch? Would tripping on the tongue produce a senseless rattling or would the ideas come across more clearly?

Read a speech slowly, taking care to make all the words. Mouth it as many of our players do. Then practice the accents so that it may be said easily but rapidly. Don't rush the pauses, but rush to them. Which method makes an audience sit up and listen? Think of a tape recording of a speech. Play it at a slower speed than it was recorded, then play it at a faster speed. Despite the distortions in pitch, isn't the faster speed easier to understand than the slower one?

These questions are asked to suggest that rapid speech can be clear and that the regular alternation of accented syllables in blank verse allows rapid, and therefore exciting speech.

This is not to argue that the Elizabethan conventions of verse speaking should be used in the modern theatre. Our actors are skillful in ways which are probably quite different from the ways Burbage and Shakespeare were skilled as actors. We are probably more careful about characterization and the subtleties of a dramatic situation. By thoughtful analysis and lengthy rehearsals we achieve effects of ensemble playing and realistic impersonation which the Elizabethan players would not have had time to perfect. Our directors and designers influence the impact of a production in ways which often place the speaking actor in a subordinate position. These conventions and practices of the modern theatre call for less rapid speech, somewhat longer psychological pauses, to use Stanislavski's term, and the development of significant stage pictures and groupings, all of which are antithetical to the conventions of a theatre which is centered on artful speech. It would be foolish to compromise these skills simply to reconstruct an obsolete convention of theatre speech.

But surely in the revival of Shakespeare's plays on the modern stage we might go further in the direction of finding methods of production more consistent with the complicated language of the plays. The freshness and spontaneity of Shakespeare's theatre might be more fully revived if the wordiness of his scripts were exploited. That means, first of all, using his verse for speed and clarity.

Another assumption of our study is open to question: that the lines were spoken as written and that the regularity of the verse was observed in production. It is possible that Shakespeare developed his varied measures and elisions as an outward conformity to the conventions of literature, but that in the theatre the Elizabethan actors regarded his lines as a basis for a somewhat improvisational style of playing, using neither his exact diction nor his carefully worked out verse. Not that they used a fully improvisational dialogue, as in the Italian *commedia dell'arte,* but neither did they go about saying only what was set down for them. Thus, although a literary study may show the lines scanning according to rules, what happened in practice may have been very different.

The veneration we hold for Shakespeare's text was probably not held by his contemporaries. And Elizabethan actors would not have been constrained, as modern actors are, to be accurate for fear of the buffs who know the lines by heart and would be thrown into a rage by an inaccurate recitation. It is difficult, too, to imagine that Shakespeare would have argued with Burbage, like a modern school master, over the accentuation of a line.

These speculations suggest that the effort to provide actors with perfected measures may have been a wasted effort, an exercise in craftsmanship that would have had little practical consequence in the theatre. But this seems at odds with the facts.

Writing blank verse is not a particularly arduous or tedious thing to do. It is no more difficult to learn how to phrase sentences that scan as blank verses than it is to learn how to spell words. It is troublesome at first, but with a little practice it becomes a part of thinking of what to write in the first place.

To return to our speculations. If the Elizabethan actors placed no exalted value on Shakespeare's exact phrasing, all his scenes might just as well have been written in prose. Unless, of course, Shakespeare were ambitious for literary fame and not content with his very real success in the theatre.

The facts of Shakespeare's life, however, suggest that he cared little for his literary as compared to his theatrical achievements. He never took the time to prepare his manuscripts for publication, but he was deeply involved in the production of his plays. His claim to status was solidly based on his position as a sharer, one of the small group of actors who controlled the affairs of The Lord Chamberlain's Men, a troupe which later came under the direct patronage of King James. His energy and labors were directed toward excelling in that position of eminence, toward making his plays contribute to theatrical events. If he ever thought of an audience made up of students of literature, it would have seemed a pale audience compared to the living and expectant one assembled at the Globe or the Blackfriars Theatre or at the court of Elizabeth or James. If the actors on those occasions did not make the effort to be faithful to his text, to exploit the verse he had provided, it doesn't seem likely that the dialogue would have been cast in verse.

If all these considerations return us to the view that Shakespeare's blank verse was used in the theatre as written, and that it was quite regular in form, then another question arises. Doesn't the regularity of verse operate as a straight jacket, dictating the precise way everything will be said? Interpretation is confined, and the actor is placed in a rigid position from which he can only escape by saying to hell with the verse, I'll have to rely on my brains, taste, and gut feelings.

Now this is an imaginary, not a real problem. When it comes to the beautiful line:

The multitudinous seas incarnadine, *Mac.* 2.2.59.

scanning tells us that *multitudinous* should be contracted to *multitud'nous.* An actor may love the polysyllabic liquidity of the word and decide to forget the verse pattern and give the word the full five syllable treatment. But the number of times such a choice can be had is rare. Verse is based on the way words are ordinarily pronounced and if we want to get away from the verse pattern, in most cases our only way out is to change the words themselves.

It is true that the arrangement of syllables in verse limits the way a line can be accented, and to that extent, limits the shades of meaning and feeling which can be conveyed by it. But this kind of limitation is imposed on an actor whenever he memorizes particular wording, whether that wording is phrased in prose or verse. If the particular dialogue seems a straight jacket, the way out is to abandon the exact wording; with few exceptions that is the only way a verse pattern can be changed.

The distinction between an accented syllable and an unaccented one which is observed in making verses is often a very slight distinction. The accentuation determined by the placement of words in phrases still leaves enormous room for the actor's interpretive contribution. As far as the pattern of accentuation goes, Hamlet's famous line can be said in two ways:

/ x
To be, or not to be, that is the question:

x /
To be, or not to be, that is the question: *Ham.* 3.1.55.

There never was and never will be an actor who, having decided between those two, would imagine that his work on the line had been completed. Beyond that choice, the voice can shade and color those words in unnumbered ways, set off the phrases by an equal variety in pause, pace, and intonation, use all the range of sound quality from piano to forte, from staccato to legato, suggesting subtleties of character, mood, and situation. With such a world of choices to be made, not to mention the matters of movement, stance, grimace, and gesture, the accentuation of words determined by their arrangement is firm ground from which to take flight rather than a straight jacket limiting the scope of an actor's interpretation.

Providing verse dialogue of service to actors, when we think of it, requires the use of a regular verse form. The principles and rules of that verse should be solidly based on the spoken language, and the rules should be as simple as possible and consistently followed. Otherwise speaking it well would require extra study and there would not be time for the more complicated matters that go to the creation of a role.

Shakespeare was an actor himself and knew what they had to do. He provided space for their contribution. He is the master playwright because he consistently leaves room for interpretation, for the collaborative art of the theatre.

VI

NOTES AND READING GUIDE

We turn'd o'er many books together.
– Merchant of Venice. 4.1.156.

1. Versification.

A thorough discussion of Shakespeare's verse will be found in E. A. Abbott, *A Shakespearian Grammar,* 1870, pages 328-429. The numerous illustrative examples in fine print are difficult to read and sometimes scanned in ways which seem arbitrary. Unfortunately he follows the old Globe text which has been outdated by modern scholarship. M. A. Bayfield, *A Study of Shakespeare's Versification,* 1920, disputes the traditional view of an iambic base for English prosody and argues that Shakespeare's lines are filled with trisyllabic and quadrisyllabic feet. He seems to regard contractions as sinful. Dorothy L. Sipe, *Shakespeare's Metrics,* 1968, demonstrates that Shakespeare invented and changed words to suit his metrical pattern rather than use a word at hand if it did not fit the regular blank verse scheme.

A fascinating study of the versification of *Macbeth* will be found in Richard Flatter, *Shakespeare's Producing Hand,* 1948. He suggests that a close look at versification will provide clues to stage business, such as asides, simultaneous speeches, pauses, and entrances.

Briefer discussions of versification will be found in F. E. Halliday, *The Poetry of Shakespeare's Plays,* 1954, a treatment in terms of literary appreciation; A. C. Partridge, *Orthography in Shakespeare and Elizabethan Drama,* 1964, a study of spelling in the early printed drama as it relates to contractions, elisions, and versification; John Russell Brown, *Shakespeare's Dramatic Style,* 1971, discusses versification briefly but the focus of the book is on an analysis of several roles.

The study of English versification in a variety of forms including blank verse can be pursued in Karl Shapiro and Robert Beum, *A Prosody Handbook,* 1965, and in G. S. Fraser, *Metre, Rhyme, and Free Verse,* 1970. Both books quote some wonderful poetry and include bibliographies for further reading.

Bertram Joseph, *Acting Shakespeare,* 1960, does not discuss versification, but it reveals much about formal rhetorical training in Renaissance times and how Shakespeare's art supports the actor in performance. The rhetorical traditions of Elizabethan writing as they relate to acting are also discussed in Ronald Watkins, *On Producing Shakespeare,* 1964, chapter 4.

2. Shakespeare's Text.

The quotations from Shakespeare used in this study and their identifying line numbers are taken from *The Riverside Shakespeare,* 1974, G. Blakemore Evans, textual editor. Whenever the scansion of a particular line of verse is to be considered, spelling and punctuation as well as the exact wording become important matters. Since most of us have neither the technical knowledge nor experience to qualify as textual critics, we have to rely on editions prepared by scholars who have spent some time acquiring that special skill. But it is not difficult to acquire enough knowledge to check their work.

Although we like to think that we are studying lines exactly as Shakespeare wrote them, the fact is that we can never be sure that a particular line is his. None of his manuscripts have survived, except for a passage in a play about Sir Thomas More which some scholars think Shakespeare had a hand in writing. The earliest printed versions of the plays could very well have a lot of material in them that Shakespeare did not write, and all sorts of minor variations from the original script.

There is no way of knowing exactly what sort of copy the type setters used in preparing the earliest printed versions. They may not have had a Shakespearean manuscript, but a copy made from the theatre prompt book, which itself may not have been the original Shakespearean manuscript but a slightly altered version of it. Everyone who works in the theatre knows how messy a prompt book can be. The copy presented to the printer may very well have been more tidy and "correct" than the manuscript Shakespeare turned over to the players. We can only guess what sort of copy the printers were using.

Editors try to guess so they can reconstruct the authentic text, that is the play as Shakespeare first wrote it. The modern actor and director would have a slightly different aim in trying to guess what sort of copy the printers were using: their aim would be to reconstruct the original prompt book. They would like to hear a performance; the editors would like to see Shakespeare's handwriting.

To understand what lies in back of a modern edition, we have to become familiar with the early printed texts which are readily available in facsimile. See *The Norton Facsimile: The First Folio of Shakespeare,* prepared by Charlton Hinman, 1968. A series of facsimiles of the quartos prepared by W. W. Greg and Charlton Hinman are available from Oxford University Press.

The punctuation and spelling of the early printed texts will seem strange at first, but these peculiarities are often suggestive. For example, in most modern editions, Macbeth's line is printed like this:

> To-morrow, and to-morrow, and to-morrow,

In the folio, the collection of Shakespeare's plays printed in 1623, the line is printed without hyphens so that *tomorrow* appears as a phrase rather than a word:

> To morrow, and to morrow, and to morrow,

While this does not change the scansion of the line, this slightly different form of the line suggests a slightly different rhythm, a suggestion that an actor would want to consider.

About half of Shakespeare's plays were printed in quarto editions before the folio collection was published. The quarto and folio texts are often different in substantial ways, as well as in minor details, and a comparison of the two texts, trying to guess which one reflects a performance more fully is a fascinating study. Hamlet's famous line appears in the quarto of 1604 as follows:

To be, or not to be, that is the question,

In the folio, the difference is in the smallest details, but suggestive:

To be, or not to be, that is the Question:

Modern editors print the line in a form that suits their sense of correctness and readability, preferring to follow modern conventions of spelling and punctuation instead of the sometimes confusing practice of Elizabethan writing and printing. And, of course, a modern editor can print the line only one way. He must make a choice. An actor would want to see both versions.

In most cases it will be seen that the modern editor has made the better choice for most editors manage to acquire an actor's ear. And in cases where neither the folio nor quarto text makes sense, the actor or director will be thankful for the emendation the editor has made by conjecture.

A full discussion of the particular textual problems of individual plays will be found in The New Cambridge and The New Arden editions. By way of introduction to the general problems of editing Shakespeare and speculations about how his plays got into print, see Alfred W. Pollard, *Shakespeare's Fight with the Pirates,* 1920, and Fredson Bowers, *On Editing Shakespeare,* 1966.

3. Pronunciation.

The authoritative modern study of Elizabethan pronunciation is Helge Kökeritz, *Shakespeare's Pronunciation,* 1953, supplemented by his *Shakespeare's Names: A Pronouncing Dictionary,* 1959, which is a handy book for actors to know. In an appendix to *Shakespeare's Pronunciation,* Kökeritz lists only 224 words which had a different accentuation from the one used in modern English. Of these only 82 are used in verse where the meter invariably requires an accentuation that would be strange to us. That is a small number when we consider the gigantic proportions of Shakespeare's vocabulary. As far as accentuation goes, Shakespearean verse simply does not present much of a problem.

On the other hand, the vowel and consonant sounds of Elizabethan English were different from modern English. When reconstructed, as on side 3 of Helge

Kökeritz, *A Thousand Years of English Pronunciation,* E A V Lexington Record no. L E 7650-7655, Shakespeare's speech sounds to us like an old fashioned country dialect, quaint and more like American than modern British speech. This suggests that the American actor who affects an English accent when playing Shakespeare is making a silly blunder. The standard pronunciation of words in modern American speech is as close to Elizabethan English, if not closer, as the speech of modern Britain.

For American productions of Shakespeare the work to consult on questions of pronunciation is Kenyon and Knott, *A Pronouncing Dictionary of American English,* 1949, not Daniel Jones, *An English Pronouncing Dictionary,* 1937.

4. Checking Accentuation.

The statistics on *revenue* are taken from Marvin Spevak, *The Harvard Concordance to Shakespeare,* 1973. This concordance, keyed to *The Riverside Shakespeare,* provides a quick way of checking the accentuation of words in Shakespeare's verse. For in addition to giving the context in which words appear, it also indicates whether the passage is in verse or prose. By scanning the verse passages, one can quickly see the accentuation of the word and, as in the case of *revenue,* some possible variations in accentuation.

5. Accent in English.

The discussion of accent presented in this study is limited to those matters which seem useful to have in mind for the purpose of scanning verse. But accent is a more complicated matter than the discussion suggests. For one thing accenting involves sustaining or lengthening vowel sounds as well as stressing or emphasizing the consonants and vowels in a syllable.

Some discussions of blank verse analyze in terms of the difference between long and short vowels, rather than the difference between accented and unaccented ones. And there is a common practice of marking vowels in verse as long or short:

Ĭf mūsĭc bē thĕ fōōd ŏf lōve, plăy ōn, *12th N.* 1.1.1.

rather than the way used in this study of marking them as accented or unaccented:

x /x / x / x / x /
If music be the food of love, play on,

Now while it is true that an accented syllable has a long vowel and an unaccented one has a short vowel, it is also true that the longer a vowel sound is sustained, the more its musical tone is apparent. Thus, if a speaker thinks of lengthening vowels, rather than of accenting syllables, he will find himself chanting. Some readers of verse cross the unmarked boundary between saying something and singing it. They intone rather than speak. They sound well, for a time, but over a long evening, their musical tones become tedious. To avoid crossing that line between chanting and speaking verse, it is important to think of accented syllables rather than of long vowels.

The distinction between the prosody of verse for singing, where long and short vowels are apparent, and the prosody of verse for speaking, where accented and unaccented syllables are apparent, is succinctly described in the "Introduction" by W. H. Auden and Chester Kallman to Greenberg, Auden, and Kallman, *An Elizabethan Song Book,* 1956, pages vii-viii. (I am indebted to Ann Hayes for bringing the "Introduction" to my attention in her unpublished lecture, "The Literary Tradition of Shakespeare's Verse: Some Elizabethan Songs," The Margery Bailey Memorial Lectures, 1971, Ashland, Oregon.)

Another feature of some accented vowels is that they tend to be spoken at a higher pitch – the natural result of increased tension in the vocal apparatus required to accent a syllable. I once heard an actor speak this line:

x / x / x /x / x /
Enrobe the roaring waters with my silks, *Merchant.* 1.1.34.

with this eccentric accentuation:

x / x / x /x x / x
Enrobe the roaring waters with my silks,

Say the line both ways and notice how the pitch of the voice has to go higher to accent the word *my*. The rise in pitch is quite noticeable in this case because ordinarily, in speaking, the end of a clause is marked by a rise in pitch on the next to last syllable. This sentence "tune" requires that *my* be sounded at a higher pitch anyway, then to have the word come across as accented, an even higher pitch has to be used.

Accent is part of the larger phonological system of our language. And to be able to understand it accurately, a more sophisticated understanding of English would be needed. This takes time, but a good place to begin the exploration would be W. Nelson Francis, *The English Language: An Introduction,* 1965, a discussion quite unlike the ordinary grammar book because it is as concerned with a description of the characteristics of our spoken language as it is with the rules of formal writing.

6. Punctuation.

Shakespeare's text is punctuated so differently in different editions that it isn't a very good idea to rely on it to settle any fine points of syntax and intonation. The opening line of *The Merchant of Venice* has only a comma by way of punctuation in the quarto of 1600 and the folio of 1623:

In sooth I know not why I am so sad,

That seems very light punctuation in comparison to modern practice. As far as I know only The New Cambridge edition, 1926, and The New Arden, 1955, allow the text to stand that way. Most modern editors punctuate more heavily. *In sooth* is followed by a comma and the line ends with a period or a semi-colon.

The reluctance of modern editors to follow the Elizabethan punctuation is understandable. Anyone can see that the conventions of Elizabethan punctuation are different from ours, but since no one has come up with an acceptable explanation of the principles that guided Elizabethan practice, if there were any generally accepted ones, it would be difficult to follow them in an edition for modern readers. A very interesting theory was presented by Percy Simpson, *Shakespeare's Punctuation,* 1911. His theory was that Elizabethan punctuation was rhythmical rather than logical, more indicative of the way a sentence is to be said than of its grammatical structure or syntax as modern punctuation tends to be. This theory led to further investigation by other scholars. Their work is critically and engagingly surveyed in Peter Alexander, *Shakespeare's Punctuation,* 1945. The result has been that modern editors look more carefully at the punctuation of the early printed versions of the plays. But they end up adopting a style of punctuation more familiar to their readers.

Those engaged in the performance or recitation of Shakespeare's verse would naturally find Dr. Simpson's theory about Elizabethan punctuation exciting. But on second thought, every actor knows that any system of punctuation can only give the roughest indication of the rhythm or intonation with which a sentence could be said. The punctuation of the Elizabethans would be suggestive, perhaps even helpful in a way modern punctuation is not, but it cannot indicate enough to determine the fine points of intonation and rhythm.

PROPERTY OF
METHODIST COLLEGE LIBRARY
FAYETTEVILLE, N. C.

The fact is that the syntax of a sentence and the way it should be said, are interrelated and inseparable. A system of punctuation cannot treat one and exclude the other. An adequate indication of syntax requires a sentence diagram. And the symbols developed by linguists to describe the phonemes, length of pause, and pitches of an utterance would have to be used to provide an adequate indication of the way a sentence is to be said. Those complex and related matters can only be indicated roughly by the handful of punctuation marks conventionally used by Elizabethan and modern printers.

7. The Run-on Line.

In many discussions of Shakespearean blank verse, the reader is told that the number of run-on lines increased substantially in the latter plays of Shakespeare which greatly increased the variety and flexibility of his verse. Indeed, verse tests, made by counting the number of run-on lines, were used by scholars in helping to fix the chronology of the plays on the theory that the larger the number of run-on lines, the more likely the play was written late in Shakespeare's career as a dramatist. In the metrical tables published in E. K. Chambers, *William Shakespeare: A Study of Facts and Problems,* 1930, for example, the early plays are listed as having a 10 to 15 per cent overflow, while his late plays have more than a 40 per cent overflow.

These facts have suggested to some that taking a pause at the end of a run-on line would go against Shakespeare's design and that treating the lines as discrete units is improper. In other words, it is argued that an actor ought not to pause at the end of a line unless a mark of punctuation is there to stop him. But it seems to me that in verse form, the lines are there for a purpose and to run lines together is to violate that purpose.

In a very interesting article, "On Reading Verse Aloud," in *The Atlantic Monthly,* CLXIV (1939), 91-95, Robert Hillyer lays it down as a rule that the last syllable of an overflowing line should be drawn out as a way of marking the end of the line without pausing. This is practical, except when the last syllable of a line is an unaccented one. Try prolonging the unaccented final syllable of these lines:

/ x x / / x x / x / (x)
Fie on't, oh fie! 'tis an unweeded garden

x / x / x / x / x /(x)
That grows to seed, things rank and gross in nature

x / x / (x)
Possess it merely. *Ham.* 1.2.135-137.

Prolonging the sound of an unaccented syllable makes it an accented one. In English a lengthened vowel is an accented one. In singing the distinction of long and short syllables is a meaningful distinction, but not in speaking English.

Another rule of Mr. Hillyer's is an excellent one: take extravagant pauses.

8. Shakespeare's Theatre.

The physical arrangement of the public stage on which Shakespeare's plays were first produced has been the subject of many studies. Two by C. Walter Hodges, *The Globe Restored,* 1953, and *Shakespeare's Second Globe,* 1973, provide stunning pictorial reconstructions as well as the relevant documentation. Leslie Hotson, *The First Night of Twelfth Night,* 1954, reconstructs a performance at court. A. M. Nagler, *Shakespeare's Stage,* 1958, gives a compact survey, including speculations on the circumstances of production.

The theatre considered in its broadest sense, as including the method of production, company organization, style of acting and dramaturgy, as well the physical building itself, is discussed in a variety of recent studies: Bernard Beckerman, *Shakespeare at the Globe,* 1962; Nevill Coghill, *Shakespeare's Professional Skills,* 1964; J. L. Styan, *Shakespeare's Stagecraft,* 1967; Ronald Watkins and Jeremy Lemmon, *The Poet's Method,* 1974.

Biographers of Shakespeare, while giving consideration to his work as a writer, tend to overlook his career in the theatre itself. Of the standard biographies, Marchette Chute, *Shakespeare of London,* 1949, gives one of the best pictures of his work in the theatre. Ivor Brown, *How Shakespeare Spent the Day,* 1963, focuses attention on Shakespeare as actor, manager, and producer.

9. Playing Time.

The figure of 1,000 lines an hour is reliable in estimating the playing time of a modern production of Shakespeare if no time is lost in shifting scenery and if dances, pantomimes, and ceremonial spectacles are held to the minimum requirements. I first noticed this while stage managing productions at the Oregon Shakespearean Festival in the 1958 season. Since then I have been able to estimate playing time by simply multiplying the number of lines by .06 to get the time of a performance in minutes. The actual playing time and the estimate have seldom varied more than 2 minutes per hour.

If a substantial part of a play is in prose, the line count may be misleading because the number of syllables in a line of prose depends on the printing format. In most editions, however, the column of print is designed to accommodate a line of verse, so a line of prose has nearly the same number of syllables. Thus the calculation of a 1,000 lines an hour is often reliable for prose as well as verse.

The full text recordings of the plays by The Shakespeare Recording Society, available through Caedmon Records, tend to take less time, but these are performances before a microphone and pauses that develop in performance before an audience do not exist.

Playing time is influenced, of course, by the style of production and acting. An interesting letter from Bernard Shaw to John Barrymore, occasioned by the London opening of Barrymore's *Hamlet* in 1925, notes that the Stratford-on-Avon Festival had produced nearly the entire play, some 3,900 lines, in 3 hours and 50 minutes. But he scolded Barrymore for cutting an hour and a half of Shakespeare's text and still taking nearly 4 hours to get through the performance because so much extra business had been interpolated. See Edwin Wilson, *Shaw on Shakespeare,* 1961, pages 95-97. Barrymore's style of speech was probably slower paced than is the fashion nowadays.

Edwin Booth's *Hamlet* of 1870 was cut to 2,752 lines and every effort was made to provide nearly instantaneous scene changes, but the production lasted 4 hours. How much time was taken for intermissions is not on record, but there is clear evidence that Booth, in common with other 19th Century actors, took a lot of time to make his points. See Charles H. Shattuck, *The Hamlet of Edwin Booth,* 1969.

A more recent example confirms my figure of 1,000 lines an hour. The Gielgud-Burton production of *Hamlet* played 3,274 lines in 3 hours and 12 minutes, about a minute less than 1,000 per hour. See Richard Stern, *John Gielgud Directs Richard Burton in Hamlet,* 1967, page 154.

Finally it should be noted that modern actors can move at a faster clip than 1,000 lines an hour. In the production of *Hamlet* by the National Theatre of Great Britain at the Old Vic in the 1975-76 season, an uncut acting text had a playing time of 3 hours and 25 minutes, that means a pace of nearly 1,200 lines an hour. See Gordon M. Wickstrom, *Educational Theatre Journal,* 28:3 (October, 1976), 421-422. Most interesting, from the standpoint of my discussion beginning on page 50 above, is the suggestion in Dr. Wickstrom's review that this production achieved its rapid pace, at least in part, by eliminating the elaborate stage business and picturesque movements characteristic of the modern theatre.